Italian Phrase book for Travelers (with audio!)

+1400 COMMON ITALIAN PHRASES to travel in Italy with confidence!

By Talk in Italian

Contents

Introduction vi

Part 1: Essentials / I fondamentali 1
   Chapter 1: The basics / Le basi 2
   Chapter 2: Difficulties / Le difficoltà 13

Part 2: Talking to people / Parlare con le persone 17
   Chapter 3: Interaction / Interazione 18
   Chapter 4: Get to know somebody – Fare conoscenza 39

Part 3: Directions, Transport…/ Indicazioni stradali, trasporti 43
   Chapter 5: Asking the way / Chiedere indicazioni 44
   Chapter 6: Bus and coach / Autobus e pullman 46
   Chapter 7: Metro / La metropolitana 48
   Chapter 8: Train – Il treno 50
   Chapter 9: Taxi – Il taxi 53
   Chapter 10: Boat and ferry / Barca e traghetto 55
   Chapter 11: Air travel / Viaggio in Aereo 57
   Chapter 12: Customs control / Controllo doganale 59
   Chapter 13: Petrol, gas / Rifornimento 60
   Chapter 14: Breakdown / In panne 61
   Chapter 15: Car parts / Pezzi di ricambio 62
   Chapter 16: Road signs / Segnali stradali 65
   Chapter 17: Signs and notices / Segnali e avvisi 67

Part 4 : Leisure, Culture and Entertainment / Tempo libero, cultura, intrattenimento 73
   Chapter 18: Sightseeing and tourist office – Ufficio turistico 74
   Chapter 19: Entertainment – Intrattenimento 76
   Chapter 20: Music – La musica 77
   Chapter 21: Cinema – Il cinema 80
   Chapter 22: Theater / opera – Il teatro e l'opera 81

Chapter 23: Television – La televisione. 83
Chapter 24: Sports – Lo sport 85
Chapter 25: Walking – La passeggiata 89
Chapter 26: Phone and Text messaging – Telefono e invio di messaggi 90
Chapter 27: E-mail. 93
Chapter 28: Internet 95
Chapter 29: Fax. 97

Part 5 : Eating and Drinking – Mangiare e bere 99
Chapter 30: Café / Restaurant Drink / Food – Il cibo 100
Chapter 31: At the restaurant / Al ristorante .102
Chapter 32: Foods / Il cibo 110
Chapter 33: Menu breakfast foods / La colazione 114
Chapter 34: Special Diets & Allergies / Dieta e Allergie 118
Chapter 35: Appetizer, soups and entrées / Antipasti, Zuppe, primi piatti. 120
Chapter 36: Vegetables and salad / Verdure e insalata. 123
Chapter 37: Fruits – Frutta 127
Chapter 38: Beverages & Drinks / Bevande. 129
Chapter 39: Desserts – Les desserts 134
Chapter 40: Bar / café. 135
Chapter 41: Reading the menu – Leggere il menu 137
Chapter 42: In a restaurant – In un ristorante 138
Chapter 43: Vegetarian / Vegetariano. 140
Chapter 44: Wines and spirits / Vino e alcolici 141

Part 6: Traveling & Planning (Trips, Weather, Activities) – Viaggi e pianificazione (meteo e attività). 143
Chapter 45: Accomodations – Alloggi 144
Chapter 46: Weather – Il meteo 153
Chapter 47: Sightseeing – Giro turistico 154
Chapter 48: Amusements – Divertimenti 158
Chapter 49: Disabled travelers / Viaggiatori disabili 162
Chapter 50: With kids – Con i bambini. 163

Contents

Part 7 : Money & Shopping – Soldi e acquisti **165**
  Chapter 51: Money / Soldi 166
  Chapter 52: Banking / La banca 167
  Chapter 53: Paying / I pagamenti.................................170
  Chapter 54: Luggage / I bagagli..................................172
  Chapter 55: Repairs / Riparazioni................................173
  Chapter 56: Laundry / Lavanderia 174
  Chapter 57: Shopping / acquisti..................................175
  Chapter 58: To Complain / Lamentarsi.............................182
  Chapter 59: Problems / Problemi 183
  Chapter 60: Emergencies / Emergenze 185

Part 8 : Health – La salute **189**
  Chapter 61: Pharmacy / La farmacia 190
  Chapter 62: Dealing with Medical Issues / Problemi di salute 191
  Chapter 63: Doctor / Il dottore 196
  Chapter 64: Dentist / Il dentista 198

Part 9: Miscellaneous / Varie **199**
  Chapter 65: Liquid / I liquidi...................................200
  Chapter 66: Quantity / Quantità..................................201
  Chapter 67: Cardinal numbers / I numeri cardinali 203
  Chapter 68: Time / L'ora 207
  Chapter 69: Days of the week / I giorni della settimana..........210
  Chapter 70: Months of the year / I mesi dell'anno 211
  Chapter 71: Seasons / Le stagioni 213
  Chapter 72: Colors & Shapes / Colori e Forme....................214
  Chapter 73: Measurements / Misure................................216

Conclusion 218
Audio Download Instructions 219
I am Here to Help 220

Introduction

You probably picked up this phrasebook for one of these reasons: a) you're starting to learn Italian and want to have a bit of a head start by learning Italian phrases, or b) you're planning to travel to Italy soon.

Whether your reason is A or B, or both, that's wonderful news. Learning Italian phrases can open so many doors for you in both instances–literally and otherwise.

Some would say that learning Italian is not a necessity when you're traveling to Italy. Yes, in fact it isn't a requirement. If you stick to the major cities, you can get by without speaking a word of Italian. But being able to speak some basic phrases will make a world of difference to your travel experience.

If you wish to have as authentic an experience as possible, learning even just a few basic phrases will help greatly.

If you want to be more than just a tourist and more of a real traveller, you need to know the most useful phrases.

You'll see the difference in how the shopkeeper, bartender, and locals will exude more warmth when you speak to them in their language. You'll see how people will brighten up at hearing you extend the courtesy of speaking to them in their language. You will have a more positive experience in your travel–that's guaranteed.

That's the aim of this book

This book wants to make your travelling experience in Italy as smooth as possible by giving you all the phrases and vocabulary you need to communicate in Italian in a simple way.

This is not a book that will teach you the entirety of the Italian language. But it is a great guide to help you navigate all kinds of scenarios during your travels in Italy: from the moment you arrive at the airport, getting about and doing touristy activities, to the more serious ones such as facing untoward events and emergencies.

Introduction

This is a book that will make you feel confident when facing any kind of scenario during your travel. Plus, it has bonus materials that will equip you with what you need to make the most of your vacation.

Here's what you'll find inside:

Part 1: Essentials / I fondamentali

Chapter 1: The basics / Le basi

This chapter will be the most useful when you need help getting out of a difficult situation.

Salve / Ciao (inf)
[cha-oh]
Hello / Hi

Arrivederci / Ciao
[cha-oh]
Goodbye/Bye

Scusi, signore / signora!
[scoo-see, see-nyoh-reh / see-nyoh-rah]
Excuse me! (to catch attention)

Mi scusi!
[mee scoo-see]
Sorry!

Mi scusi
[mee scoo-see]
Excuse me

Mi dispiace
[mee dees-pyah-cheh]
I am sorry

Grazie (mille)
[grah-tzyeh (meel-leh)]
Thanks (very much)

Per favore
[pehr fah-voh-reh]
Please

Lei parla inglese?
[Leh-ee pahr-lah een-gleh-seh]
Do you speak English?

Qualcuno qui parla inglese?
[Qwahl-coo-noh qwee pahr-lah een-gleh-seh]
Does anyone here speak English?

Io parlo solo inglese
[ee-oh pahr-loh soh-loh een-gleh-seh]
I speak only English

Io parlo un po' l'italiano
[ee-oh pahr-loh oon poh ee-tah-lyah-noh]
I speak a little Italian

La prego, parli più lentamente
[lah preh-goh, pahr-lee pyoo lehn-tah-mehn-teh]
Please speak more slowly

Io (non) capisco
[ee-oh (nohn) cah-pees-coh]
I (do not) understand

Mi capisce?
[mee cah-pee-sheh]
Do you understand me?

Può ripetere per favore?
[pwoh ree-peh-teh-reh, pehr fah-voh-reh]
Could you repeat it, please?

Lo scriva, per favore
[Loh scree-vah, pehr fah-voh-reh]
Write it down, please

Cosa significa questo?
[Coh-sah see-nyee-fee-cah qwes-toh]
What does this mean?

Prego / Di nulla
[Preh-goh / Dee nul-lah]
You are welcome

Come si dice «xx» in italiano?
[coh-meh see dee-cheh "xx" een ee-tah-lyah-noh]
How do you say "xx" in Italian?

Come si scrive "xx"?
[coh-meh see scree-veh "xx"]
How do you write "xx"?

Può farmi lo spelling di "xx"?
[pwoh fahr-mee loh spehl-leeng dee "xx"]
Can you spell "xx"?

Cos'è quello?
[coh-seh qwel-loh]
What is that?

No
[noh]
No

Forse
[fohr-seh]
Perhaps

Sì
[see]
Yes

Sono un cittadino degli Stati Uniti d'America
[soh-noh oon chee-tah-dee-noh deh-lee stah-tee oo-nee-tee dah-meh-ree-cah]
I am a United States citizen

Il mio indirizzo (di posta) è XX
[eel mee-oh een-dee-reet-zoh (dee pohs-stah) eh XX]
My (mailing) address is XX

Cosa desidera?
[coh-zah deh-see-deh-rah]
What do you wish?

Venga qui / Vieni qui (inf)
[vehn-gah qwee / vee-eh-nee qwee]
Come here

Entri / Entrate (pl)
[ehn-tree / ehn-trah-teh]
Come in

Attenda un momento / Aspetti un attimo
[att-tehn-dah oon moh-mehn-toh]
Wait a moment

Vado di fretta
[vah-doh dee fret-tah]
I am in a hurry

Ho caldo, freddo
[hoh cahl-doh, freh-doh]
I am warm, cold

Ho fame, sete
[hoh fah-meh, seh-teh]
I am hungry, thirsty

Sono occupato, stanco
[soh-noh oh-coo-pah-toh, stahn-coh]
I am busy, tired

Mi fa piacere / Sono lieto
[mee fah pya-cheh-reh / soh-noh lee-eh-toh]
I am glad

Che c'è? / Che succede?
[keh cheh / keh sooh-cheh-deh]
What is the matter here?

Va tutto bene
[vah tooh-toh beh-neh]
It is all right

Io (non) lo so
[ee-oh (nohn) loh soh]
I (do not) know

Io (non) credo
[ee-oh (nohn) creh-doh]
I (do not) think so

Non fa niente / non importa
[nohn fah nee-ehn-teh / nohn eem-pohr-tah]
It doesn't matter

Quant'è?
[qwan-teh]
How much is it?

È tutto
[eh toot-toh]
That is all

Può aiutarmi (dirmi)?
[pwoh ah-yoo-tahr-mee (deer-mee)]
Can you help me (tell me)?

Dov'è il bagno?
[doh-veh eel bah-nyoh]
Where is the washroom?

Il bagno degli uomini
[eel bah-nyoh deh-lee wo-mee-nee]
The men's room

Il bagno delle donne
[eel bah-nyoh deh-leh don-neh]
The ladies room

Sto cercando il mio albergo (hotel)
[stoh cher-cahn-doh eel mee-oh ahl-behr-goh (hotel)]
I am looking for my hôtel

Vorrei andarci a piedi
[voh-reh-ee ahn-dahr-chee ah pee-eh-dee]
I would like to walk there

Perché?
[pehr-keh]
Why?

Quando?
[qwan-doh]
When?

Chi?
[kee]
Who?

Cosa?
[coh-sah]
What?

Come?
[coh-meh]
How?

Quanto tempo?
[qwahn-toh tem-poh]
How long?

Quanto dista?
[qwahn-toh dees-tah]
How far?

Qui
[qwee]
Here

Lì / Là
[lee / lah]
There

A
[ah]
To

Da
[dah]
From

Con
[kohn]
With

Senza
[sehn-zah]
Without

Dentro / In / Nel (m) / Nella (f) / Nello (m)
[dehn-troh / een / nehl / neh-lah / neh-loh]
In

Sopra
[soh-prah]
On

Vicino
[vee-chee-noh]
Near

Lontano
[lohn-tah-noh]
Far

Davanti
[dah-vahn-tee]
In front of

Dietro
[dee-eh-troh]
Behind

Accanto
[ah-kahn-toh]
Beside

All'interno
[ahl-een-tehr-noh]
Inside

All'esterno
[ahl-ehs-tehr-noh]
Outside

Vuoto
[voo-oh-toh]
Empty

Pieno
[pee-eh-noh]
Full

Qualcosa
[qwal-coh-sah]
Something

Niente
[nee-ehn-teh]
Nothing

Parecchio
[pah-reh-kyoh]
Several

Poco
[poh-coh]
Few

(Molto) di più
[(mohl-toh) dee pyoo]
(Much) more

Meno
[meh-noh]
Less

(Poco) di più
[(poh-coh) dee pyoo]
(A little) more

Basta
[bah-stah]
Enough

Troppo
[troh-poh]
Too much

Tanto
[tahn-toh]
Many

Buono / Bene
[Bwoh-noh / beh-neh]
Good

Più buono (di) / migliore (di)
[pyoo bwoh-noh (dee) / mee-lyoh-reh (dee)]
Better (than)

Il migliore
[eel mee-lyoh-reh]
The Best

Cattivo
[cah-tee-voh]
Bad

Peggio (di) / peggiore (di)
[peh-djoh (dee) / peh-djoh-reh (dee)]
Worse (than)

Adesso
[ah-deh-soh]
Now

Subito
[soo-bee-toh]
Immediately

Presto
[preh-stoh]
Soon

Più tardi
[pyoo tahr-dee]
Later

Il prima possibile
[eel pree-mah poh-see-bee-leh]
As soon as possible

È (troppo) tardi
[eh (troh-poh) tahr-dee]
It is (too) late

È presto
[eh preh-stoh]
It is early

Lentamente
[lehn-tah-mehn-teh]
Slowly

Più lentamente
[pyoo lehn-tah-mehn-teh]
Slower

Velocemente
[veh-loh-cheh-mehn-teh]
Quickly

Più veloce
[pyoo veh-loh-cheh]
Faster

Attenzione!
[ah-tehn-zyoh-neh]
Look on!

Ascolti / Ascolta (inf)
[ah-scohl-tee / ah-scohl-tah]
Listen

Guardi qui / Guarda qui (inf)
[gwahr-dee qwee / gwahr-dah qwee]
Look here

Comprende? / Capisci? (inf)
[com-prehn-deh / cah-pee-shee]
Do you understand?

Cosa significa (XX)?
[coh-sah see-nee-fee-cah (XX)]
What does (XX) mean?

Come...?
[coh-meh]
How do you ...?

...si pronuncia questo
[see proh-noon-cha qwes-toh]
pronounce this

...si scrive (Buongiorno)
[see scree-veh (bwon-johr-noh)]
write (Buongiorno)

Chapter 2: Difficulties / Le difficoltà

Non riesco a trovare l'indirizzo del mio albergo
[nohn ree-eh-scoh ah troh-vah-reh leen-dee-reet-zoh dehl mee-oh ahl-behr-goh]
I cannot find my hotel address

Ho perso i miei amici
[oh pehr-soh ee mee-eh-ee ah-mee-chee]
I have lost my friends

Ho lasciato il mio portafoglio in albergo
[oh lah-shah-toh eel myoh pohr-tah-foh-lyo een ahl-behr-goh]
I left my purse, wallet in the hotel

Ho dimenticato i soldi, le chiavi
[oh dee-mehn-tee-cah-toh ee sohl-dee, leh kyah-vee]
I forgot my money, keys

Ho perso il mio treno
[oh pehr-soh eel myoh treh-noh]
I have missed my train

Cosa devo fare?
[coh-sah deh-voh fah-reh]
What am I to do?

I miei occhiali sono rotti
[ee mee-eh-ee oh-kyah-lee soh-noh roh-tee]
My glasses are broken

Dove posso farli riparare?
[doh-ve poh-soh fahr-lee ree-pah-rah-reh]
Where can they be repaired?

Un apparecchio acustico
[oon ah-pah-reh-kyoh ah-coo-stee-coh]
A hearing aid

Ufficio oggetti smarriti
[oof-fee-choh oh-djet-tee smah-ree-tee]
The lost and found desk

Il consolato americano
[eel cohn-soh-lah-toh ah-meh-ree-cah-noh]
The American consulate

L'ambasciata Americana
[lahm-bah-shah-tah ah-me-ree-cah-nah]
The American embassy

Il commissariato di polizia
[eel com-miss-sah-ryah-toh dee poh-lee-zee-ah]
The police station

Chiamerò un poliziotto
[kyah-meh-roh oon poh-lee-zyoh-toh]
I will call a policeman

Sono stato derubato.
[soh-noh stah-toh deh-roo-bah-toh]
I've been robbed.

Ho perso ...
[oh pehr-soh...]
I've lost ...

Mi hanno rubato ...
[mee ah-noh roo-bah-toh...]
... was/were stolen.

il mio zaino
[eel mee-oh zah-ee-noh]
my backpack

le mie valigie
[leh mee-eh vah-lee-djeh]
my bags

la mia carta di credito
[lah mee-ah cahr-tah dee creh-dee-toh]
my credit card

la mia borsa
[lah mee-ah bohr-sah]
my handbag

i miei gioielli
[ee mee-eh-ee jo-yell-lee]
my jewellery

i miei soldi
[ee mee-eh-ee sohl-dee]
my money

il mio passaporto
[eel mee-oh pahs-sah-pohr-toh]
my passport

i miei traveller cheque
[ee mee-eh-ee trah-veh-lehr che-k]
my travellers cheques

il mio portafoglio
[eel mee-oh pohr-tah-foh-lyoh]
my wallet

Vorrei contattare...
[voh-reh-ee cohn-tah-tah-reh…]
I want to contact…

il mio consolato
[eel mee-oh cohn-soh-lah-toh]
my consulate

la mia ambasciata
[lah mee-ah ahm-bah-shah-tah]
my embassy

Part 2: Talking to people / Parlare con le persone

Chapter 3: Interaction / Interazione

The main point of speaking Italian is to use the language in everyday conversation. As intimidating as it can be to converse in a different language, this is the ultimate goal of your studies. It is a good idea to have some basic phrases up your sleeve for when you are having conversations with people in Italian. These handy conversation starters and tips are ideal for those times when you need something relevant to say to keep the dialogue going.

Per favore
[pehr fah-voh-reh]
Please

Grazie (mille)
[grah-tsyeh (meel-leh)]
Thanks (very much)

Prego!
[preh-goh]
You're welcome!

Sì
[see]
Yes

No
[noh]
No

Sì, grazie
[see, grah-tsyeh]
Yes, please

No, grazie
[no, grah-tsyeh]
No, thanks

Ok! / Va bene
[oh-keh-ee / vah beh-neh]
OK!

Signor / Sig.
[see-nyor]
Sir/Mr

Signora / Sig.ra
[see-nyoh-rah]
Madam/Mrs/Ms

Signorina
[see-nyoh-ree-nah]
Miss

Salve / Ciao
[sahl-veh / cha-oh]
Hello/Hi

Arrivederci / Ciao
[Ah-ree-veh-dehr-chee / cha-oh]
Goodbye/Bye

Ci vediamo
[chee veh-dyah-moh]
Bye for now

Buon giorno
[bwon djohr-noh]
Good morning

Buona sera
[bwoh-nah seh-rah]
Good evening

Buona notte
[bwoh-nah not-teh]
Good night

A domani
[ah doh-mah-nee]
See you tomorrow

Mi scusi!
[mee scoo-see]
Excuse me! (to catch attention)

Mi scusi! / Chiedo scusa!
[mee scoo-see / kee-eh-doh scoo-sah]
Sorry!

Mi dispiace
[mee dees-pyah-cheh]
I'm sorry

Come va?
[coh-meh vah]
How are you?

Bene, grazie
[beh-neh, grah-tsyeh]
Fine, thanks

E lei / tu (inf)?
[eh leh-ee / too]
And you?

Io non capisco
[ee-oh nohn cah-pees-coh]
I don't understand

Parlo molto poco l'italiano
[pahr-loh mohl-toh poh-coh lee-tah-lyah-noh]
I speak very little Italian

Posso...?
[pohs-soh]
Can I...?

Fumare
[foo-mah-reh]
smoke

Il pasto era delizioso
[eel pahs-toh eh-rah deh-lee-tsyoh-soh]
The meal was delicious

Grazie mille
[grah-tsyeh meel-leh]
Thank you very much

Come ti chiami?
[coh-meh tee kyah-mee]
What's your name?

Mi chiamo...
[mee kyah-moh...]
My name is...

Piacere di conoscerti!
[pyah-cheh-reh dee coh-noh-sher-tee]
Pleased to meet you!

Piacere di conoscerla
[pyah-cheh-reh dee coh-noh-sher-lah]
Delighted to meet you

Questo/questa è...
[qwes-toh/qwes-tah eh...]
This is...

mio marito/mia moglie
[myoh mah-ree-toh / myah moh-lyeh]
my husband/my wife

Buone vacanze!
[bwoh-neh vah-cahn-tzeh]
Enjoy your holiday!

Qual è il suo / tuo (inf)
[qwal eh eel soo-oh / too-oh]
What's your …?

Indirizzo
[een-dee-ree-tsoh]
address

indirizzo e-mail
[een-dee-ree-tsoh ee-meh-eel]
email address

numero di fax
[noo-meh-roh dee fax]
fax number

numero di telefono
[noo-meh-roh dee the-leh-foh-noh]
phone number

Che lavoro fa / fai (inf)?
[keh lah-voh-roh fah / fah-ee]
What's your occupation?

Sono un / una (f)
[soh-noh oon / oon-ah…]
I'm a/an …

Di dove sei?
[dee doh-veh seh-ee]
Where are you from?

Sono inglese, vengo da Londra
[soh-noh een-gleh-seh, vehn-goh dah lohn-drah]
I am English, from London

Da dove viene / vieni (inf)?
[dah doh-veh vee-eh-neh / vee-eh-nee]
Where are you from?

Vengo..
[vehn-goh…]
I'm …

...dall'Australia
[dah-lah-oo-strah-lee-ah]
from Australia

…dal Canada
[dahl cah-nah-dah]
from Canada

…dall'Inghilterra
[dahl-een-gyeel-tehr-rah]
from England

...dalla Nuova Zelanda
[dah-lah nwoh-vah zeh-lahn-dah]

from New Zealand

...dagli Stati Uniti
[dah-lee stah-tee oo-nee-tee]
from the USA

Lei è sposato / sposata? (m/f)
[leh-ee eh spoh-sah-toh / spoh-sah-tah]
Are you married?

Sei sposato / sposata ? (m/f) inf
[seh-ee spoh-sah-toh / spoh-sah-tah]
Are you married?

Sono sposato / sposata (m/f)
[soh-noh spoh-sah-toh / spoh-sah-tah]
I'm married.

Sono single.
[soh-noh seen-gohl]
I'm single.

Quanti anni...
[qwan-tee ahn-nee]
How old …?

ha lei?
[ah le-ee]
are you

hai tu? (inf)
[ah-ee too]
are you

ha sua figlia?
[ah soo-ah fee-lya]
is your daughter

ha suo figlio?
[ah soo-oh fee-lyoh]
is your son

Ho ... anni
[hoh… ahn-nee]
I'm … years old

Ha ... anni
[hah… ahn-nee]
He/She is … years old

Io (non) sono
[ee-oh (nohn) soh-noh]
I'm (not) …

Lei è...?/ Tu sei...? (inf)
[leh-ee eh / too seh-ee]
Are you …?

Fidanzato
[fee-dahn-zah-toh]
boyfriend

fratello
[frah-tehl-loh]
brother

figlia
[fee-lya]
daughter

padre
[pah-dreh]
father

amico/amica (m/f)
[ah-mee-coh / ah-mee-cah]
friend

fidanzata
[fee-dahn-zah-tah]
girlfriend

marito
[mah-ree-toh]
husband

madre
[mah-dreh]
mother

compagno / compagna (m/f)
[cohm-pah-nyoh / cohm-pah-nyah]
partner

sorella
[soh-reh-lah]
sister

figlio
[fee-lyoh]
son

moglie
[moh-lee-eh]
wife

Questo è...
[qwes-toh eh...]
Here's...

mio fratello
[mee-oh frah-teh-loh]
My brother

il mio amico / la mia amica (m/f)
[eel mee-oh ah-mee-coh / lah mee-ah ah-mee-cah]
My friend

mia moglie
[mee-ah moh-lee-eh]
My wife

mio marito
[mee-oh mah-ree-toh]
My husband

mia sorella
[mee-ah soh-rehl-lah]
My sister

mia figlia
[mee-ah fee-lyah]
My daughter

mio figlio
[mee-oh fee-lyoh]
My son

il mio bambino
[eel mee-oh bahm-bee-noh]
My child

Il ragazzo
[eel rah-gah-tsoh]
The boy

La ragazza
[lah rah-gah-tsah]
The girl

L'uomo
[lwo-moh]
The man

La donna
[lah dohn-nah]
The woman

Felice
[feh-lee-cheh]
happy

triste
[tree-steh]
sad

freddo / fredda (m/f)
[freh-doh/freh-dah]
cold

caldo / calda (m/f)
[cahl-doh/cahl-dah]
hot

affamato / affamata (m/f)
[ah-fah-mah-toh/ah-fah-mah-tah]
hungry

assetato / assetata (m/f)
[ah-seh-tah-toh/ah-seh-tah-tah]
thirsty

Lei parla inglese? (pol)
[leh-ee pahr-lah een-gleh-seh]
Do you speak English?

Parli inglese? (inf)
[pahr-lee een-gleh-seh]
Do you speak English?

Qualcuno qui parla inglese?
[qwal-coo-noh qwee pahr-lah een-gleh-seh]
Does anyone here speak English?

Io parlo solo inglese
[ee-oh pahr-loh soh-loh een-gleh-seh]
I speak only English

Io parlo un po' l'italiano
[ee-oh pahr-loh oon poh lee-tah-lyah-noh]
I speak a little Italian

La prego, parli più lentamente
[lah preh-goh, pahr-lee pyoo lehn-tah-mehn-teh]
Please speak more slowly

Mi capisce?
[mee cah-pee-sheh]
Do you understand me?

Può ripetere per favore?
[pwoh ree-peh-the-reh, pehr fah-voh-reh]
Repeat It, please

Lo scriva, per favore
[loh scree-vah, pehr fah-voh-reh]
Write it down, please

Cosa significa questo?
[coh-sah see-nyee-fee-cah qwes-toh]
What does this mean?

Prego / Di nulla
[preh-goh/dee nuhl-lah]
You are welcome

Come si dice «xx» in italiano?
[coh-meh see dee-cheh "xx" een ee-tah-lyah-noh]
How do you say "xx" in Italian?

Come si scrive «xx»?
[coh-meh see scree-veh "xx"]
How do you write "xx"?

Può farmi lo spelling di "xx"?
[pwoh fahr-mee loh speh-leeng dee "xx"]
How do you spell "xx"?

Cos'è quello?
[coh-seh qwel-loh]
What is that?

Forse
[fohr-seh]
Perhaps

Sono un cittadino degli Stati Uniti d'America
[soh-noh oon cheet-tah-dee-noh deh-lee stah-tee oo-nee-tee dah-meh-ree-cah]
I am a United States citizen

Il mio indirizzo (di posta) è XX
[eel mee-oh een-dee-ree-tsoh (dee poh-stah) eh XX]
My (mailing) address is XX

Cosa desidera?
[coh-sah deh-see-deh-rah]
What do you wish?

Venga qui / Vieni qui (inf)
[vehn-gah qwee / vyeh-nee qwee]
Come here

Entri / Entrate (pl)
[ehn-tree / ehn-trah-teh]
Come in

Attenda un momento/ Aspetti un attimo
[ah-tehn-dah oon moh-mehn-toh/ah-speht-tee oon aht-tee-moh]
Wait a moment

Vado di fretta
[vah-doh dee freh-tah]
I am in a hurry

Ho caldo, freddo
[oh cahl-doh, freh-doh]
I am warm, cold

Ho fame, sete
[ho fah-meh, seh-teh]
I am hungry, thirsty

Sono occupato, stanco
[soh-noh oh-cooh-pah-toh, stahn-coh]
I am busy, tired

Mi fa piacere / Sono lieto
[mee fah pyah-cheh-reh/soh-noh lyeh-toh]
I am glad

Che c'è? / Che succede?
[keh cheh/keh soo-cheh-deh]
What is the matter here?

Va tutto bene
[vah toot-toh beh-neh]
It is all right

Io (non) lo so
[ee-oh (nohn) loh soh]
I (do not) know

Io (non) credo
[ee-oh (nohn) creh-doh]
I (do not) think so

Non fa niente / non importa
[nohn fah nee-ehn-teh/nohn eem-pohr-tah]
It doesn't matter

Quant'è?
[qwan-teh]
How much is it?

È tutto
[eh toot-toh]
That is all

Può aiutarmi (dirmi)?
[pwoh ah-yoo-tahr-mee (deer-mee)]
Can you help me (tell me)?

Dov'è il bagno?
[doh-veh eel bah-nyoh?]
Where is the washroom?

Il bagno degli uomini
[eel bah-nyoh deh-lee wo-mee-nee]
The men's room

Il bagno delle donne
[eel bah-nyoh deh-leh doh-neh]
The ladies room

Sto cercando il mio albergo (hotel)
[stoh chehr-cahn-doh eel myoh ahl-behr-goh (hotel)]
I am looking for my hôtel

Vorrei andarci a piedi
[voh-reh-ee ahn-dahr-chee ah pyeh-dee]
I would like to walk there

Perché?
[pehr-keh]
Why?

Quando?
[qwan-doh]
When?

Chi?
[kee]
Who?

Cosa?
[coh-sah]
What?

Come?
[coh-meh]
How?

Quanto tempo?
[qwahn-toh them-poh]
How long?

Quanto dista?
[qwahn-toh dees-tah]
How far?

Qui
[qwee]
Here

Lì / Là
[lee/lah]
There

A
[ah]
To

Da
[dah]
From

Con
[cohn]
With

Senza
[sehn-zah]
Without

Dentro / In / Nel (m) / Nella (f) / Nello (m)
[dehn-troh / een / nehl / nehl-la /nehl-lo]
In

Sopra
[soh-prah]
On

Vicino
[vee-chee-noh]
Near

Lontano
[lohn-tah-noh]
Far

Davanti
[dah-vahn-tee]
In front of

Dietro
[dee-eh-troh]
Behind

Accanto
[ah-kahn-toh]
Beside

All'interno
[ahl-een-tehr-noh]
Inside

All'esterno
[ahl-eh-stehr-noh]
Outside

Vuoto
[voo-oh-toh]
Empty

Pieno
[pyeh-noh]
Full

Qualcosa
[qwal-coh-sah]
Something

Niente
[nyehn-teh]
Nothing

Parecchio
[pah-rehk-kee-oh]
Several

Poco
[poh-coh]
Few

(Molto) di più
[(mohl-toh) dee pyoo]
(Much) more

Meno
[meh-noh]
Less

(Poco) di più
[(poh-coh) dee pyoo]
(A little) more

Basta
[bah-stah]
Enough

Troppo
[trohp-poh]
Too much

Tanto
[tahn-toh]
Many

Buono / Bene
[beh-neh]
Good

Più buono (di) / migliore (di)
[pyoo bwoh-noh (dee)/mee-lyoh-reh (dee)]
Better (than)

Il migliore
[eel mee-lyoh-reh]
The Best

Cattivo
[cah-tee-voh]
Bad

Peggio (di) / peggiore (di)
[peh-djoh (dee) / peh-djoh-reh (dee)]
Worse (than)

Adesso
[ah-dehs-soh]
Now

Subito
[soo-bee-toh]
Immediately

Presto
[preh-stoh]
Soon

Più tardi
[pyoo tahr-dee]
Later

Il prima possibile
[eel pree-mah poh-see-bee-leh]
As soon as possible

È (troppo) tardi
[eh troh-poh tahr-dee]
It is (too) late

È presto
[eh prehs-toh]
It is early

Lentamente
[lehn-tah-mehn-teh]
Slowly

Più lentamente
[pyoo lehn-tah-mehn-teh]
Slower

Velocemente
[veh-loh-cheh-mehn-teh]
Quickly

Più veloce
[pyoo veh-loh-cheh]
Faster

Attenzione!
[ah-tehn-tzyoh-neh]
Look out!

Ascolti / Ascolta (inf)
[ah-scohl-tee / ah-scohl-tah]
Listen

Guardi qui / Guarda qui (inf)
[gwar-dee qwee / gwar-dah qwee]
Look here

Come...?
[coh-meh]
How do you …?

...si pronuncia questo
[see proh-noon-cha qwe-stoh]
pronounce this

...si scrive (Buongiorno)
[see scree-veh (bwon-johr-noh)]
write (Buongiorno)

Potrebbe...?
[poh-treh-beh]
Could you…?

Per favore… ?
[pehr fah-voh-reh]
please …?

Ripeterlo ?
[ree-peh-tehr-loh]
…repeat that

Vorrei augurarle / vorrei augurarti (inf)
[vohr-rey ah-oo-goo-rahr-leh / vohr-rey ah-oo-goo-rahr-tee]
I'd like to wish you...

Felice anno nuovo!
[feh-lee-cheh ahn-noh nwo-voh]
Happy New Year!

Buona Pasqua!
[bwoh-nah pahs-qwah]
Happy Easter!

Buon compleanno!
[bwon cohm-pleh-ahn-noh]
Happy birthday!

Buon Viaggio!
[bwon vyah-joh]
Have a good trip!

Buon appetito!
[bwon ah-peh-tee-toh]
Enjoy your meal!

Chapter 4: Get to know somebody – Fare conoscenza

Quanti anni ha?
[qwahn-tee ahn-nee ah]
How old are you?

Quanti anni hai? (inf)
[qwahn-tee ahn-nee ha-ee]
How old are you?

Io ho … anni
[ee-oh hoh… ahn-nee]
I'm … years old

Lei è italiano/italiana (m/f)?
[leh-ee eh ee-tah-lyah-noh/ee-tah-lyah-nah]
Are you Italian?

Sei italiano/italiana (m/f)? (inf)
[seh-ee ee-tah-lyah-noh/ee-tah-lyah-nah]
Are you Italian?

Io sono Inglese/Scozzese/Americano
[ee-oh soh-noh een-gleh-seh/scoh-tzeh-seh/ah-meh-ree-cah-noh]
I'm English/Scottish/American

Dove vive?
[doh-veh vee-veh]
Where do you live?

Dove vivi? (inf)
[doh-veh vee-vee]
Where do you live?

Dove vivete? (pl)
[doh-veh vee-veh-teh]
Where do you live?

Io vivo a Londra
[ee-oh vee-voh ah lohn-drah]
I live in London

Noi viviamo a Glasgow
[noh-ee vee-vee-ah-moh ah glas-gow]
We live in Glasgow

Io sono…
[ee-oh soh-noh…]
I'm…

Single
[seen-gohl]
single

sposato / a (m/f)
[spoh-sah-toh]
married

divorziato / a (m/f)
[dee-vohr-tsyah-toh]
divorced

Io (non) ho…
[ee-oh (nohn) hoh…]
I have (not)…

un ragazzo
[oon rah-gah-tsoh]
a boyfriend

una ragazza
[oonah rah-gah-tsah]
a girlfriend

compagno / compagna (m/f)
[cohm-pah-nyoh/cohm-pah-nyah]
a partner (male/female)

… figli
[fee-lee]
… children

Non ho figli
[nohn hoh fee-lee]
I have no children

Sono qui in vacanza / per affari / per il fine settimana
[soh-noh qwee een vah-cahn-tsah/pehr ah-fah-ree/pehr eel fee-neh seht-tee-mah-nah]
I'm here on holiday/on business/for the weekend

Che lavoro fa?
[keh lah-voh-roh fah]
What work do you do?

Che lavoro fai? (inf)
[keh lah-voh-roh fah-ee]
What work do you do?

Io sono…
[ee-oh soh-noh…]
I'm…

un medico
[oon meh-dee-coh]
a doctor

un manager
[oon mah-nah-jer]
a manager

un segretario / una segretaria (m/f)
[oon seh-greh-tah-ryoh/oo-nah seh-greh-tah-ryah]
a secretary

Lavoro da casa
[lah-voh-roh dah cah-sah]
I work from home

Sono un lavoratore autonomo
[soh-noh oon lah-voh-rah-toh-reh ah-oo-toh-noh-moh]
I'm self-employed

Part 3: Directions, Transport…/ Indicazioni stradali, trasporti

There is nothing worse than feeling lost, let alone being lost in a foreign country. Learning Italian has, of course, some very practical uses when you are in Italy. When travelling, having a basic understanding of how to ask for directions or simply knowing the words for public transportation can make all the difference in your experience.

Chapter 5: Asking the way / Chiedere indicazioni

Mi scusi, come si arriva alla stazione?
[mee scoo-see, coh-meh see ah-ree-vah ahl-lah stah-tsyoh-neh]
Excuse me, how do I get to the station?

Prosegua dritto, dopo la chiesa a sinistra/destra
[proh-seh-gwah dreet-toh, doh-poh lah kee-eh-sah ah see-nees-trah/dehs-trah]
Keep straight on, after the church turn left/right

È lontano?
[eh lohn-tah-noh]
Is it far?

No, 200 metri/ cinque minuti
[noh, doo-eh-chen-toh meh-tree/cheen-qweh mee-noo-tee]
No, 200 yards/five minutes

Grazie!
[grah-tsyeh]
Thank you!

Noi stiamo cercando...
[noh-ee stee-ah-moh cher-cahn-doh]
We're looking for…

Possiamo andarci a piedi?
[pohs-see-ah-moh ahn-dahr-cee ah pyeh-dee]
Can we walk there?

Ci siamo persi
[cee see-ah-moh pehr-see]
We're lost

È questa la direzione giusta per..?
[eh qwes-tah lah dee-reh-tsee-oh-neh djoos-tah pehr]
Is this the right way to…?

Può indicarmelo sulla cartina?
[pwoh een-dee-cahr-meh-loh sool-lah cahr-tee-nah]
Can you show me on the map?

C'è la segnaletica
[cheh lah seh-nyah-leh-tee-cah]
It's signposted

È all›angolo della strada
[eh ahl-lahn-goh-loh dehl-lah strah-dah]
It's on the corner of the street

E' laggiù
[eh lah-djoo]
It's over there

Di fronte a
[dee fron-teh ah]
opposite of

Accanto a
[ah-cahn-toh]
next to

Vicino a
[vee-chee-noh ah]
near to

Incrocio
[een-croh-tchoh]
crossroad

Rotatoria
[roh-tah-toh-ryah]
roundabout

Chapter 6: Bus and coach / Autobus e pullman

Mi scusi, quale autobus porta in centro?
[mee scoo-see, qwah-leh ah-oo-toh-boos pohr-tah een chen-troh]
Excuse me, which bus goes to the centre?

il 780
[eel seht-teh-chen-toh-oh-tahn-tah]
Number 780

Dov'è la fermata dell'autobus?
[doh-veh lah fehr-mah-tah dehl-lah-oo-toh-boos]
Where is the bus stop?

Lì, sulla sinistra
[lee, sool-lah see-nees-trah]
There, on the left

Dove posso comprare i biglietti per l'autobus?
[doh-veh pohs-soh cohm-prah-reh ee bee-lee-eht-tee pehr lah-oo-toh-boos]
Where can I buy bus tickets?

Lì giù, alla biglietteria automatica
[lee joo, ahl-lah bee-lee-eht-teh-ree-ah ah-oo-toh-mah-tee-cah]
Over there, at the ticket machine

C'è un autobus per..?
[cheh oon ah-oo-toh-boos pehr]
Is there a bus to…?

Dove posso prendere l'autobus per..?
[doh-veh pohs-soh prehn-deh-reh lah-oo-toh-boos pehr]
Where do I catch the bus to go to…?

Quanto costa andare..?
[qwan-toh coh-stah ahn-dah-reh]
How much is it to…?

...in centro
[een chen-troh]
to the centre

...in spiaggia
[een spya-jya]
to the beach

... al centro commerciale
[ahl chen-troh com-mehr-cha-leh]
to the shops

... al Colosseo
[ahl coh-lohs-seh-oh]
...to the Colosseum

Ogni quanto passano gli autobus per...?
[oh-nyee qwahn-toh pahs-sah-noh lee ah-oo-toh-boos pehr]
How frequent are the buses to…?

Quando parte il primo/l'ultimo autobus per...?
[qwahn-doh pahr-teh eel pree-moh/lool-tee-moh ah-oo-toh-boos pehr]
When is the first/the last bus to…?

Può dirmi quando scendere?
[pwoh deer-mee qwahn-doh shehn-deh-reh]
Could you tell me when to get off?

Questa è la mia fermata
[qwehs-stah eh lah mee-ah fehr-mah-tah]
This is my stop

Prenda la metropolitana, è più veloce
[prehn-dah lah meh-troh-poh-lee-tah-nah, eh pyoo veh-loh-cheh]
Take the metro, it's quicker

Chapter 7: Metro / La metropolitana

Entrata
[ehn-trah-tah]
entrance

Uscita
[oo-shee-tah]
way out/exit
sor-tee

Linea della Metropolitana
[lee-neh-ah dehl-lah meh-troh-poh-lee-tah-nah]
metro line

Direzione…
[dee-reh-tsyo-neh]
in the direction of…

Linea di collegamento
[lee-neh-ah dee cohl-leh-gah-mehn-toh]
connecting line

Dov'è la fermata della metro più vicina?
[doh-veh lah fehr-mah-tah dehl-lah meh-troh pyoo vee-chee-nah]
Where is the nearest metro?

Sto andando a…
[stoh ahn-dahn-doh ah]
I'm going to…

Come funziona la biglietteria automatica?
[coh-meh foon-tsyo-nah lah bee-lee-eht-teh-ree-ah ah-oo-toh-mah-tee-cah]
How does the ticket machine work?

Avete una cartina della metropolitana?
[ah-veh-teh oo-nah cahr-tee-nah dehl-lah meh-troh-poh-lee-tah-nah]
Do you have a map of the metro?

Come posso arrivare a...?
[coh-meh pohs-soh ah-ree-vah-reh ah]
How do I get to…?

Devo cambiare?
[deh-voh cahm-byah-reh]
Do I have to change?

Quale è la linea per?
[qwah-leh eh lah lee-neh-ah pehr]
Which line is it for…?

In quale direzione?
[een qwah-leh dee-reh-tsyoh-neh]
In which direction?

Qual è la prossima fermata?
[qwah-leh lah proh-see-mah fehr-mah-tah]
What is the next stop?

Chapter 8: Train – Il treno

Orari
[oh-rah-ree]
timetable

Domenica e festivi
[doh-meh-nee-cah eh feh-stee-vee]
Sundays and holidays

Ai binari
[ah-ee bee-nah-ree]
access to the platforms

Quando parte il prossimo treno per...?
[qwhan-doh pahr-teh eel proh-see-moh treh-noh pehr]
When is the next train to…?

Alle cinque e dieci
[ahl-le cheen-qweh eh dee-eh-chee]
At ten past five

Due biglietti per...
[doo-eh bee-lee-eh-tee pehr]
Two tickets to…

Solo andata o andata e ritorno?
[soh-loh ahn-dah-tah oh ahn-dah-tah eh ree-tohr-noh]
Single or return?

Prima classe / seconda classe
[pree-mah clah-seh/seh-cohn-dah clah-seh]
First class/Second class

Fumatori / Non fumatori
[foo-mah-toh-ree/nohn foo-mah-toh-ree]
Smoking/Non-smoking

C'è un supplemento da pagare?
[cheh oon soop-leh-mehn-toh dah pah-gah-reh]
Is there a supplement to pay?

Vorrei un biglietto per il Frecciarossa per Milano
[voh-reh-ee oon bee-lee-eh-toh pehr eel freht-cha-rohs-sah pehr mee-lah-noh]
I want to book a seat on the Frecciarossa to Milan

Quando parte il treno per...?
[qwahn-doh pahr-teh eel treh-noh pehr]
When is the train to…?

Quando parte?
[qwahn-doh pahr-teh]
When does it leave?

il primo/l'ultimo
[eel pree-moh/lool-tee-moh]
the first/the last

A che ora arriva a...?
[ah keh oh-rah ah-ree-vah ah]
When does it arrive in…?

Devo cambiare?
[deh-voh cahm-byah-reh]
Do I have to change?

A quale binario parte?
[ah qwah-leh bee-nah-ree-oh pahr-teh]
Which platform does it leave from?

Questo è il binario per il treno per Roma?
[qwes-toh eh eel bee-nah-ree-oh pehr eel treh-noh pehr roh-mah]
Is this the right platform for the train to Rome?

Questo è il treno per...?
[qwes-toh eh eel treh-noh pehr]
Is this the train for…?

Il treno ferma a...?
[eel treh-noh fehr-mah ah]
Does the train stop at…?

Dove posso cambiare per...?
[doh-veh pohs-soh cahm-byah-reh pehr]
Where do I change for…?

Per favore, può avvisarmi quando arriviamo a...?
[pehr fah-voh-reh, pwoh ah-vee-sahr-mee qwan-doh ah-ree-vyah-moh ah]
Please tell me when we get to…

Questo posto è libero?
[qwes-toh poh-stoh eh lee-beh-roh]
Is this seat free?

Mi scusi
[mee scoo-see]
Excuse me

Mi scusi!
[me scoo-see]
Sorry!

Chapter 9: Taxi – Il taxi

La stazione dei taxi
[lah stah-tsyoh-neh deh-ee tah-xee]
taxi rank

Vorrei un taxi
[voh-reh-ee oon tah-xee]
I want a taxi

Dove posso prendere un taxi?
[doh-veh pohs-soh prehn-deh-reh oon tah-xee]
Where can I get a taxi?

Potrebbe chiamarmi un taxi?
[poh-trehb-beh kee-ah-mahr-mee oon tah-xee]
Could you order me a taxi?

Quanto costerà andare...?
[qwahn-toh coh-steh-rah ahn-dah-reh]
How much is it going to cost to go to…?

in centro
[een chen-troh]
to the town centre

in stazione
[een stah-tsyoh-neh]
to the station

all'aeroporto
[ahl-lah-eh-roh-pohr-toh]
to the airport

a questo indirizzo
[ah qwehs-toh een-dee-reet-tsoh]
to this address

Quanto costa?
[qwahn-toh coh-stah]
How much is it?

Tenga il resto
[tehn-gah eel reh-stoh]
Keep the change

Mi scusi, non ho il resto
[mee scoo-see, nohn oh eel reh-stoh]
Sorry, I don't have any change

Vado di fretta
[vah-doh dee freht-tah]
I'm in a hurry

È lontano?
[eh lohn-tah-noh]
Is it far?

Chapter 10: Boat and ferry / Barca e traghetto

Quando parte il prossimo traghetto per...?
[qwahn-doh pahr-the eel proh-see-moh trah-gueh-toh pehr]
When is the next boat/ferry to…?

Avete gli orari?
[ah-veh-teh lee oh-rah-ree]
Have you a timetable?

C'è un traghetto per auto per...?
[cheh oon trah-gueh-toh pehr ah-oo-toh pehr]
Is there a car ferry to…?

Quanto costa un biglietto di sola andata?
[qwahn-toh coh-stah oon bee-lee-eh-toh dee soh-lah ahn-dah-tah]
How much is a single?

Quanto costa un biglietto andata e ritorno?
[qwahn-toh coh-stah oon bee-lee-eh-toh ahn-dah-tah eh ree-tohr-noh]
How much is a return ?

Un biglietto turistico
[oon bee-lee-eh-toh too-rees-tee-coh]
A tourist ticket

Quanto costa imbarcare un'auto e ... persone?
[qwahn-toh coh-stah eem-bahr-cah-reh oon-ah-oo-toh eh ... pehr-soh-neh]
How much is it for a car and … people?

Quanto dura la traversata?
[qwahn-toh doo-rah lah trah-vehr-sah-tah]
How long is the crossing?

Da dove parte la barca?
[dah doh-veh pahr-teh lah bahr-cah]
Where does the boat leave from?

Quando parte la prima/l'ultima barca?
[qwahn-doh pahr-teh lah pree-mah/lool-tee-mah bahr-cah]
When is the first/last boat?

A che ora arriviamo a...?
[ah keh oh-rah ahr-ree-vyah-moh ah]
What time do we get to…?

C'è un posto dove mangiare sulla barca?
[cheh oon poh-stoh doh-veh mahn-djah-reh sool-lah bahr-cah]
Is there somewhere to eat on the boat?

Chapter 11: Air travel / Viaggio in Aereo

Come posso raggiungere l'aeroporto?
[coh-meh pohs-soh rah-djoon-djeh-reh lah-eh-roh-pohr-toh]
How do I get to the airport?

Quanto tempo ci vuole per raggiungere l'aeroporto?
[qwahn-toh tem-poh chee voo-oh-leh pehr rah-djoon-djeh-reh lah-eh-roh-pohr-toh]
How long does it take to get to the airport?

Quanto costa il taxi fino...?
[qwahn-toh coh-stah eel tah-xee fee-noh]
How much is the taxi fare…?

in città
[een cheet-tah]
into town

all'albergo
[ahl-ahl-behr-goh]
to the hotel

C'è una navetta per andare in centro?
[cheh oo-nah nah-veht-tah pehr ahn-dah-reh een chen-troh]
Is there an airport bus to the city centre?

Dove posso fare il check in?
[doh-veh pohs-soh fah-reh eel check-een]
Where do I check in for…?

Dove sono i bagagli del volo da...?
[doh-veh soh-noh ee bah-gah-lee dehl voh-loh dah]
Where is the luggage for the flight from…?

Da quale gate parte il volo per...?
[dah qwah-leh gate pahr-the eel voh-loh pehr]
Which is the departure gate for the flight to…?

L'imbarco avverrà al gate numero...
[leem-bahr-coh ah-veh-rah ahl gate noo-meh-roh]
Boarding will take place at gate number...

Vada subito al gate numero...
[vah-dah soo-bee-toh ahl gate noo-meh-roh]
Go immediately to gate number...

Il suo volo è in ritardo
[eel soo-oh voh-loh eh een ree-tahr-doh]
Your flight is delayed

Chapter 12: Customs control / Controllo doganale

controllo del passaporto
[kohn-trohl-loh dehl pah-sah-pohr-toh]
passport control

UE (Unione Europea)
[oo-eh (oo-nyo-neh eh-oo-roh-peh-ah]
EU (European Union)

altri passaporti
[ahl-tree pah-sah-pohr-tee]
other passports

dogana
[doh-gah-nah]
customs

Devo pagare una tassa per questo?
[deh-voh-pah-gah-reh oo-nah tahs-sah pehr qwes-toh]
Do I have to pay duty on this?

È per uso personale
[eh pehr oo-soh pehr-soh-nah-leh]
It is for my own personal use

Stiamo andando a...
[stee-ah-moh ahn-dahn-doh ah]
We are on our way to…(if in transit through a country)

Chapter 13: Petrol, gas / Rifornimento

Benzina senza piombo
[behn-zee-nah sehn-tsah pyom-boh]
unleaded

diesel
[dee-sehl]
diesel

Il pieno, per favore
[eel pee-eh-noh, pehr fah-voh-reh]
Fill it up, please

Può controllare l'olio/l'acqua per favore?
[pwoh cohn-trohl-lah-reh loh-lee-oh/lah-qwah, pehr fah-voh-reh]
Please check the oil/the water

... euro di benzina senza piombo
[... eh-oo-roh dee behn-zee-nah sehn-tsah pyom-boh]
…euros' worth of unleaded petrol

Pompa di benzina numero...
[pohm-pah dee behn-zee-nah noo-meh-roh...]
Pump number…

Può controllare la pressione delle gomme?
[pwoh cohn-trohl-lah-reh lah press-see-oh-neh dehl-leh gohm-meh]
Can you check the tyre pressure?

Dove posso pagare?
[doh-veh pohs-soh pah-gah-reh]
Where do I pay?

Accettate carte di credito?
[ah-tchet-tah-teh cahr-teh dee creh-dee-toh]
Do you take credit cards?

Chapter 14: Breakdown / In panne

Assistenza in caso di guasto
[ah-see-stehn-zah een cah-soh dee gwah-stoh]
Breakdown assistance

Può aiutarmi?
[pwoh ah-yoo-tahr-mee]
Can you help me?

La mia auto è in panne
[lah mee-ah ah-oo-toh eh een pahn-neh]
My car has broken down

Non riesco a far partire l'auto
[nohn ree-eh-scoh ah fahr pahr-tee-reh lah-oo-toh]
I can't start the car

Ho finito la benzina
[oh fee-nee-toh lah behn-zee-nah]
I've run out of petrol

C'è un'officina qui vicino?
[cheh oon-off-fee-chee-nah qwee vee-chee-noh]
Is there a garage near here?

Può rimorchiarmi all'officina più vicina?
[pwoh ree-mohr-kyahr-mee ahl-off-fee-chee-nah pyoo vee-chee-nah]
Can you tow me to the nearest garage?

Avete dei pezzi di ricambio per una...?
[ah-veh-the deh-ee peh-tsee dee ree-cahm-byoh pehr oon-ah]
Do you have parts for a (make of car)?

C'è qualcosa che non va con il/la/lo...
[cheh qwal-coh-sah keh nohn vah cohn eel/lah/loh]
There's something wrong with the...

Chapter 15: Car parts / Pezzi di ricambio

Il/lo/la... non funziona
[eel/loh/lah... nohn foon-tsyoh-nah]
The ... doesn't work

I/Le... non funzionano
[ee/leh nohn foon-tsyoh-nah-noh]
The ... don't work

l'acceleratore
[lah-tche-leh-rah-toh-reh]
accelerator

la batteria
[lah baht-teh-ree-ah]
battery

il cofano
[eel coh-fah-noh]
bonnet

i freni
[ee freh-nee]
brakes

lo starter
[loh stahr-tehr]
choke

la frizione
[lah free-tsyoh-neh]
clutch

il motore
[eel moh-toh-reh]
engine

il tubo di scarico
[eel too-boh dee scah-ree-coh]
exhaust pipe

il fusibile
[eel foo-see-bee-leh]
fuse

ingranaggi
[een-grah-nah-djee]
gears

il freno a mano
[eel freh-noh ah mah-noh]
handbrake

i fari
[ee fah-ree]
headlights

l'accensione
[lah-tchen-tsyoh-neh]
ignition

il lampeggiante
[eel lahm-peh-djahn-teh]
clignotant

il radiatore
[eel rah-dyah-toh-reh]
radiator

luci di retromarcia
[loo-chee dee reh-troh-mahr-cha]
reversing lights

cintura di sicurezza
[cheen-too-rah dee see-coo-reh-tsah]
seat belt

luci di posizione
[loo-chee dee poh-see-tsyoh-neh]
sidelights

ruota di scorta
[roo-oh-tah dee scohr-tah]
spare wheel

candele
[cahn-deh-leh]
spark plugs

sterzo
[stehr-tsoh]
steering

volante
[voh-lahn-teh]
steering wheel

lo pneumatico
[loh pneh-oo-mah-tee-coh]
tyre

ruota
[roo-oh-tah]
wheel

parabrezza
[pah-rah-breh-tsah]
windscreen

rondelle del parabrezza
[rohn-dehl-leh dehl pah-rah-breh-tsah]
windscreen washers

tergicristallo
[tehr-gee-kree-stahl-loh]
windscreen wiper

Chapter 16: Road signs / Segnali stradali

Dogana
[doh-gah-nah]
Customs

stazione di pedaggio per l'autostrada
[stah-tsyoh-neh dee peh-dah-djoh pehr lah-oo-toh-strah-dah]
toll station for motorway

dare la precedenza
[dah-reh lah preh-cheh-dehn-tsah]
give way

rallentare
[rahl-lehn-tah-reh]
slow down

senso unico
[sehn-soh oo-nee-coh]
one way

deviazione
[deh-vee-ah-tsyoh-neh]
diversion priority road

Nord
[nord]
North

Sud
[sood]
South

Ovest
[oh-vehst]
West

Est
[ehst]
East

Libero
[lee-beh-roh]
spaces

pieno
[pyeh-noh]
full

divieto di parcheggio
[dee-vee-eh-toh dee pahr-ke-djoh]
no parking

accendere i fari
[ah-tchen-deh-reh ee fah-ree]
switch on your light

autostrada
[ah-oo-toh-strah-dah]
motorway

Chapter 17: Signs and notices / Segnali e avvisi

Ingresso
[een-grehs-soh]
entrance

uscita
[oo-shee-tah]
exit

aperto
[ah-pehr-toh]
open

chiuso
[kee-oo-soh]
closed

caldo
[cahl-doh]
hot

freddo
[freh-doh]
cold

tirare
[tee-rah-reh]
pull

spingere
[speen-dje-reh]
push

destra
[deh-strah]
right

sinistra
[see-nee-strah]
left

acqua potabile
[ah-qwah poh-tah-bee-leh]
drinking water

da asporto/ da portar via
[dah ah-spohr-toh/dah pohr-tahr vee-ah]
take-away

degustazione di vini
[deh-goo-stah-tsyoh-neh dee vee-nee]
wine tasting

si prega di...
[see preh-gah dee]
please...

libero
[lee-beh-roh]
free, vacant

occupato
[oh-coo-pah-toh]
engaged

cassa
[cahs-sah]
cash desk

bagni
[bah-nyee]
toilets

donne
[dohn-neh]
ladies

uomini
[woh-mee-nee]
gents

fuori servizio
[fwoh-ree sehr-vee-tsyoh]
out of order

in affitto/ a noleggio
[een ah-feet-toh]
for hire/to rent

in vendita
[een vehn-dee-tah]
for sale

divieto di balneazione
[dee-vee-eh-toh dee bahl-neh-ah-tsyoh-neh]
no bathing

seminterrato
[seh-meen-teh-rah-toh]
basement

piano terra
[pyah-noh tehr-rah]
ground floor

ascensore
[ah-shen-soh-reh]
lift

accesso ai treni
[ah-ches-soh ah-ee treh-nee]
access to the trains

camere disponibili
[cah-meh-reh dees-poh-nee-bee-lee]
rooms available

al completo
[ahl cohmp-leh-toh]
no vacancies

uscita di emergenza
[oo-shee-tah dee eh-mehr-djehn-tsah]
emergency exit

suonare
[soo-oh-nah-reh]
ring

premere
[preh-meh-reh]
press

privato
[pree-vah-toh]
private

stop
[stohp]
stop

biglietti
[bee-lee-eht-tee]
tickets

informazioni (pl)
[een-for-mah-tsyoh-nee]
information

convalida il tuo biglietto
[cohn-vah-lee-dah eel too-oh bee-lee-eh-toh]
validate your ticket

snack
[snehk]
snacks

deposito bagagli
[deh-poh-see-toh bah-gah-lyee]
left luggage

non fumatori
[nohn foo-mah-toh-ree]
non-smoking

fumatori
[foo-mah-toh-ree]
smoking

vietato fumare
[vee-eh-tah-toh foo-mah-reh]
no smoking

Part 4 : Leisure, Culture and Entertainment / Tempo libero, cultura, intrattenimento

One of the wonderful aspects of learning a language is the cultural immersion and the experiences you gain from it. Italian culture has a wealth of connections to leisure and entertainment, which can really enhance your level of enjoyment when learning the language. When you take your interests, such as sports or the arts, and apply to them to learning Italian, you will find that you are more motivated and interested in increasing your knowledge about that topic while also learning the language along the way.

Chapter 18: Sightseeing and tourist office – Ufficio turistico

Dov'è l'ufficio turistico?
[doh-veh loof-fee-tcho too-rees-tee-coh]
Where is the tourist office?

Cosa c'è da visitare nella zona?
[coh-sah cheh dah vee-see-tah-reh nehl-lah zoh-nah]
What is there to visit in the area?

in ... ore
[een… oh-reh]
in … hours

Avete dei volantini?
[ah-veh-the deh-ee voh-lahn-tee-nee]
Do you have any leaflets?

Ci sono delle escursioni?
[chee soh-noh dehl-leh eh-scoor-see-oh-nee]
Are there any excursions?

Vorremmo andare a...
[voh-reh-moh ahn-dah-reh ah]
We'd like to go to…

Quanto costa entrare?
[qwahn-toh coh-stah ehn-trah-reh]
How much does it cost to get in?

Ci sono riduzioni per...?
[chee soh-noh ree-doo-tsyoh-nee pehr]
Are there any reductions for…?

i bambini
[ee bahm-bee-nee]
children

gli studenti
[lee stoo-dehn-tee]
students

i disoccupati
[ee dee-soh-coo-pah-tee]
the unemployed

gli anziani
[lee ahn-tsyah-nee]
senior citizens

Chapter 19: Entertainment – Intrattenimento

Cosa c'è da fare la sera?
[coh-sah cheh dah fah-reh lah seh-rah]
What is there to do in the evenings?

Avete una lista di eventi per questo mese?
[ah-veh-teh oo-nah lees-tah dee eh-vehn-tee pehr qwes-toh meh-seh]
Do you have a list of events for this month?

C'è qualcosa da fare per i bambini?
[cheh qwal-coh-sah dah fah-reh pehr ee bahm-bee-nee]
Is there anything for children to do?

Dove posso/possiamo...?
[doh-veh pohs-soh/pohs-see-ah-moh]
Where can I/we...?

andare a pesca
[ahn-dah-reh ah pehs-cah]
go fishing

andare a cavallo
[ahn-dah-reh ah cah-vahl-loh]
go riding

Ci sono delle buone spiagge qui vicino?
[chee soh-noh dehl-leh bwoh-neh spee-ah-djeh qwee vee-chee-noh]
Are there any good (sandy) beaches near here?

C'è una piscina?
[cheh oo-nah pee-shee-nah]
Is there a swimming pool?

Chapter 20: Music – La musica

Ci sono dei buoni concerti?
[chee soh-noh deh-ee bwoh-nee cohn-cher-tee]
Are there any good concerts on?

Dove posso acquistare i biglietti per il concerto?
[doh-veh pohs-soh ah-qwee-stah-reh ee bee-lee-eh-tee pehr eel cohn-cher-toh]
Where can I get tickets for the concert?

Dove possiamo ascoltare della musica classica/del jazz?
[doh-veh pohs-see-ah-moh ah-scohl-tah-reh dehl-lah moo-see-cah clah-see-cah/dehl jazz]
Where can we hear some classical music/some jazz?

Mi piace ascoltare musica
[mee pyah-cheh ah-scohl-tah-reh moo-see-cah]
I love listening to music

Che genere di musica ascolti?
[keh djeh-neh-reh dee moo-see-cah ah-scohl-tee]
What kind of music do you listen to?

Sono un musicista
[soh-noh oon moo-see-chee-stah]
I'm a musician

Io suono…
[ee-oh soo-oh-noh]
I play

il pianoforte
[eel pyah-noh-fohr-teh]
the piano

Il pianoforte a coda
[eel pyah-noh-fohr-teh ah coh-dah]
grand piano

la chitarra classica
[lah kee-tahr-rah clah-see-cah]
classical guitar

la chitarra elettrica
[lah kee-tahr-rah eh-let-tree-cah]
electric guitar

il violino
[eel vee-oh-lee-noh]
violin

il violoncello
[eel vee-oh-lohn-chel-loh]
cello

il mandolino
[eel mahn-doh-lee-noh]
mandolin

l'arpa
[lahr-pah]
harp

la batteria
[lah baht-teh-ree-ah]
drums

il basso
[eel bahs-soh]
bass guitar

il contrabbasso
[eel cohn-trah-bah-soh]
double bass

il fagotto
[eel fah-goht-toh]
bassoon

il flauto
[eel flah-oo-toh]
flute

il clarinetto
[eel clah-ree-neht-toh]
clarinet

il sassofono
[eel sahs-soh-foh-noh]
saxophone

la tromba
[lah trohm-bah]
trumpet

Io sono direttore d'orchestra
[ee-oh soh-noh dee-reht-toh-reh dohr-keh-strah]
I'm a conductor

Io canto
[ee-oh cahn-toh]
I sing

Sono un/una cantante
[soh-noh oon/oo-nah cahn-tahn-teh]
I'm a singer

Chapter 21: Cinema – Il cinema

Sottotitolato
[soht-toh-tee-toh-lah-toh]
subtitled

spettacolo
[speht-tah-coh-loh]
performance

in lingua originale (non doppiato)
[een leen-gwa oh-ree-jee-nah-leh (nohn dop-pyah-toh)]
in the original language (i.e. not dubbed)

Cosa c'è al cinema?
[coh-sah cheh ahl chee-neh-mah]
What's on at the cinema?

Quando inizia/finisce il film?
[qwahn-doh ee-nee-tsya/fee-nee-sheh eel feel-m]
When does the film start/finish?

Quanto costano i biglietti?
[qwahn-toh coh-stah-noh ee bee-lee-eh-tee]
How much are the tickets?

Vorrei due posti da ... euro
[vohr-re-ee doo-eh poh-stee dah... eh-oo-roh]
I'd like two seats at ... euros

Chapter 22: Theater / opera – Il teatro e l'opera

lo spettacolo
[loh speht-tah-coh-loh]
play

lo spettacolo
[loh speht-tah-coh-loh]
performance

in platea
[een plah-teh-ah]
in the stalls

in galleria
[een gahl-leh-ree-ah]
in the circle

il posto/ la poltrona
[eel poh-stoh/lah pohl-troh-nah]
seat

il guardaroba
[eel-gwar-dah-roh-bah]
cloakroom

intervallo
[een-tehr-vahl-loh]
interval

Cosa c'è a teatro / all'opera?
[coh-sah cheh ah teh-ah-troh/ahl-loh-peh-rah]
What is on at the theatre/at the opera?

Quanto costano i biglietti?
[qwahn-toh coh-stah-noh ee bee-lee-eh-tee]
What prices are the tickets?

Vorrei due biglietti...
[voh-reh-ee doo-eh bee-lee-eh-tee]
I'd like two tickets…

per questa sera
[pehr qwes-tah seh-rah]
for tonight

per domani sera
[pehr doh-mah-nee seh-rah]
for tomorrow night

per il cinque Agosto
[peh eel cheen-qweh ah-goh-stoh]
for 5th August

Quando inizia/finisce lo spettacolo?
[qwahn-doh ee-nee-tsyah/fee-nee-sheh loh speht-tah-coh-loh]
When does the performance begin/end?

Chapter 23: Television – La televisione

Telecomando
[teh-leh-coh-mahn-doh]
remote control

Telenovela/Soap Opera
[teh-leh-noh-veh-lah/ soap opera]
Soap

Notiziario
[noh-tee-tsyah-ree-oh]
News

Accendere
[ah-tchen-deh-reh]
to switch on

spegnere
[speh-nee-eh-reh]
to switch off

i cartoni animati
[ee cahr-toh-nee ah-nee-mah-tee]
cartoons

Dov'è la televisione?
[doh-veh lah teh-leh-vee-see-oh-neh]
Where is the television?

Come si accende?
[coh-meh see ah-tchen-deh]
How do you switch it on?

Cosa c'è in televisione?
[coh-sah cheh een teh-leh-vee-see-oh-neh]
What is on television?

A che ora c'è il notiziario?
[ah ke oh-rah cheh eel noh-tee-tsyah-ree-oh]
When is the news?

Avete dei canali in lingua inglese?
[ah-veh-teh deh-ee cah-nah-lee een leen-gwah een-gleh-seh]
Do you have any English-language channels?

Avete dei video in Inglese?
[ah-veh-teh deh-ee vee-deh-oh een een-gleh-seh]
Do you have any English videos?

Chapter 24: Sports – Lo sport

Dove posso/possiamo...?
[doh-veh pohs-soh/pohs-see-ah-moh]
Where can I/we…?

giocare a calcio
[djoh-cah-reh ah cahl-tcho]
play soccer

giocare a tennis
[djoh-cah-reh ah ten-nees]
play tennis

giocare a golf
[djoh-cah-reh ah golf]
play golf

nuotare
[nwoh-tah-reh]
go swimming

fare jogging
[fah-reh jogging]
go jogging

Qual è il costo orario?
[qwal-eh eel coh-stoh oh-rah-ree-oh]
How much is it per hour?

Bisogna essere soci?
[bee-soh-nya ehs-seh-reh soh-chee]
Do you have to be a member?

Possiamo noleggiare...?
[pohs-see-ah-moh noh-leh-djah-reh]
Can we hire…?

Racchette
[rahk-keht-teh]
Rackets

mazze da golf
[mah-tseh dah golf]
golf clubs

Vorremmo andare a vedere la ... giocare
[voh-rehm-moh ahn-dah-reh ah veh-deh-reh lah… djoh-cah-reh]
We'd like to go to see (name of team) play

Dove posso/possiamo prendere i biglietti?
[doh-veh pohs-soh/pohs-syah-moh prehn-deh-reh ee bee-lee-eh-tee]
Where can I/we get tickets?

Non ci sono più biglietti per la partita
[nohn chee soh-noh pyoo bee-lee-eh-tee pehr lah pahr-tee-tah]
There are no tickets left for the game

Quale sport pratichi?
[qwa-leh sport prah-tee-kee]
What sports do you play?

tiro con l'arco
[tee-roh cohn lahr-coh]
archery

ciclismo
[cheek-lees-moh]
cycling

pallavolo
[pahl-lah-voh-loh]
volleyball

pallacanestro
[pahl-lah-cah-neh-stroh]
basketball

freccette
[freh-tcheh-teh]
darts

sci
[shee]
skiing

palla
[pahl-lah]
ball

scacchi
[scah-kee]
chess

dama
[dah-mah]
draughts

carte
[cahr-teh]
cards

cuori
[qwoh-ree]
hearts

fiori
[fyoh-ree]
clubs

picche
[peek-keh]
spades

quadri
[qwah-dree]
diamonds

tocca a te
[toh-kah ah teh]
your turn

gioco da tavolo
[djoh-coh dah tah-voh-loh]
board game

gioco
[djoh-coh]
game

partita
[pahr-tee-tah]
match

punteggio
[poon-teh-djoh]
score

vincitore
[veen-chee-toh-reh]
winner

arbitro
[ahr-bee-troh]
referee

Chapter 25: Walking – La passeggiata

Ci sono delle passeggiate guidate?
[chee soh-noh dehl-leh pahs-seh-djah-teh gwee-dah-teh ?]
Are there any guided walks?

Avete una guida per le passeggiate locali?
[ah-veh-teh oo-nah gwee-dah pehr leh pahs-seh-djah-teh loh-cah-lee ?]
Do you have a guide to local walks?

Conoscete dei bei percorsi?
[coh-noh-sheh-teh deh-ee beh-ee pehr-cohr-see]
Do you know any good walks?

Di quanti chilometri è la passeggiata?
[dee qwahn-tee kee-loh-meh-tree eh lah pahs-seh-djah-tah]
How many kilometres is the walk?

Quanto tempo ci vuole?
[qwahn-toh tehm-poh chee voo-oh-leh]
How long will it take?

È molto ripido?
[eh mohl-toh ree-pee-doh ?]
Is it very steep?

Vorremmo fare una scalata
[vohr-rehm-moh fah-reh oo-nah scah-lah-tah]
We'd like to go climbing

Chapter 26: Phone and Text messaging – Telefono e invio di messaggi

Vorrei fare una telefonata
[vohr-reh-ee fah-reh oo-nah teh-leh-foh-nah-tah]
I'd like to make a phone call

C'è un telfono pubblico ?
[cheh oon teh-leh-foh-noh poob-lee-coh]
Is there a pay phone?

Una scheda telefonica, per favore
[oo-nah skeh-dah teh-leh-foh-nee-cah, pehr fah-voh-reh]
A phonecard, please

di ... euro
[dee ... e-oo-roh]
for ... euros

Ha un cellulare?
[hah oon chel-loo-lah-reh]
Do you have a mobile?

Qual è il suo numero di cellulare?
[qwal eh eel soo-oh noo-meh-roh dee chel-loo-lah-reh]
What's your mobile number?

Posso usare il suo cellulare?
[pohs-soh oo-sah-reh eel soo-oh chel-loo-lah-reh]
Can I use your mobile?

Il mio numero di cellulare è...
[eel mee-oh noo-meh-roh dee chel-loo-lah-reh eh...]
My mobile number is...

Pronto?
[prohn-toh]
Hello

Chapter 26: Phone and Text messaging – Telefono e invio di messaggi

Con chi parlo?
[cohn kee pahr-loh]
Who's calling?

Sono...
[soh-noh]
This is…

Un momento...
[oon moh-mehn-toh]
Just a moment…

Posso parlare con...?
[pohs-soh pahr-lah-reh cohn]
Can I speak to…?

Come ottengo la linea esterna?
[coh-meh oh-tehn-goh lah lee-neh-ah eh-stehr-nah]
How do I get an outside line?

Richiamo...
[ree-kee-ah-moh]
I'll call back…

più tardi
[pyoo tahr-dee]
later

domani
[doh-mah-nee]
tomorrow

glielo/gliela passo (m/f)
[lyeh-loh/lyeh-lah pahs-soh]
I'm putting you through

È occupato
[eh oh-coo-pah-toh]
It's engaged

Può provare a chiamare più tardi?
[pwoh proh-vah-reh ah kee-ah-mah-reh pyoo tahr-dee]
Please try later?

Vuole lasciare un messaggio?
[voo-oh-leh lah-shah-reh oon meh-sah-djoh]
Do you want to leave a message?

Si prega di lasciare un messaggio dopo il segnale acustico
[see preh-gah dee lah-sha-reh oon meh-sah-djoh doh-poh eel seh-nyah-leh ah-coos-tee-coh]
Please leave a message after the tone

Si prega di spegnere il cellulare
[see preh-gah dee speh-nyeh-reh eel chel-loo-lah-reh]
Please turn your mobile off

Ti scrivo / Ti mando un messaggio
[tee scree-voh/tee mahn-doh oon meh-sah-djoh]
I will text you

Mi puoi mandare un messaggio?
[mee poo-oh-ee mahn-dah-reh oon meh-sah-djoh]
Can you text me?

Chapter 27: E-mail

Nuovo Messaggio:
[noo-oh-voh meh-sah-djo]
New message:

A:
[ah]
To:

Da:
[dah]
From:

Oggetto:
[oh-djeh-toh]
Subject:

CC (copia conoscenza):
[chee-chee]
CC:

CCN (copia conoscenza nascosta):
[chee-chee-ehn-neh]
BCC:

Allegato:
[ahl-leh-gah-toh]
Attachment:

Invia:
[een-vee-ah]
Send:

Rispondi
[rees-pohn-dee]
Reply

Ha un indirizzo mail?
[hah oon een-dee-ree-tso meh-eel]
Do you have an e-mail address?

Qual è il suo indirizzo mail?
[qwal eh eel soo-oh een-dee-ree-tso meh-eel]
What's your e-mail address?

Può fare lo spelling?
[pwoh fah-reh loh spehl-leeng]
How do you spell it?

Tutto attaccato
[toot-toh ah-tah-cah-toh]
All in one word

Tutto minuscolo
[toot-toh mee-noos-coh-loh]
All lower case

Il mio indirizzo mail...
[eel mee-oh een-dee-ree-tsoh meh-eel]
My e-mail address is…

Chiocciola
[kee-oh-tchoh-lah]
@

xxpuntoxxchiocciola....punto it
[xx poon-toh xx kee-oh-tchoh-lah… poon-toh eet]
XX.XX@(company name).it

Posso inviare una mail?
[pohs-soh een-vee-ah-reh oo-nah meh-eel]
Can I send an e-mail?

Ha ricevuto la mia mail?
[hah ree-cheh-voo-toh lah mee-ah meh-eel]
Did you get my e-mail?

Chapter 28: Internet

Home
[hom]
Home

username
[yuu-sehr-neh-eem]
username

motore di ricerca
[moh-toh-reh dee ree-chehr-cah]
search engine

password
[pahs-sword]
password

contattaci
[cohn-tah-tah-chee]
contact us

torna al menu
[tohr-nah ahl meh-noo]
back to menu

indietro
[een-dee-eh-troh]
back

Ci sono degli Internet café qui?
[chee soh-noh deh-lee een-tehr-neht cah-feh qwee]
Are there any internet cafés here?

Quanto costa connettersi per un'ora?
[qwahn-toh coh-stah cohn-neh-tehr-see pehr oon oh-rah]
How much is it to log on for an hour?

Non riesco a connettermi
[nohn ree-eh-scoh ah cohn-neh-tehr-mee]
I can't log on

Accedi
[ah-tcheh-dee]
Log in

Esci
[eh-shee]
Log out

Chapter 29: Fax

A/Da
[ah/dah]
To/From

Oggetto
[oh-djet-toh]
Re:

Numero di pagine
[noo-meh-roh dee pah-jee-neh]
Number of pages

Voglia trovare in allegato...
[voh-lya troh-vah-reh een ahl-leh-gah-toh]
Please find attached…

Avete un fax?
[ah-veh-teh oon fax]
Do you have a fax?

Vorrei mandare un fax
[vohr-reh-ee mahn-dah-reh oon fax]
I want to send a fax

Qual è il suo numero di fax?
[qwah-leh eel soo-oh noo-meh-roh dee fax]
What is your fax number?

Il mio numero di fax è...
[eel mee-oh noo-meh-roh dee fax eh]
My fax number is…

(non) inviato
[(nohn) een-veeh-ah-toh]
(not) sent

Part 5 : Eating and Drinking – Mangiare e bere

One of the best ways to enjoy life is to indulge in food and drink. It is a happy occurrence when you are able to do this while learning a language. Once you have learned some basic Italian vocabulary and phrases related to eating and drinking, you can reward yourself with a trip to an Italian restaurant or café to put these skills to good use. Even better, if you get the chance to go to an Italian speaking country, you will find that this vocabulary comes in very handy.

Chapter 30: Café / Restaurant Drink / Food – Il cibo

il barman / il bartender
[eel bahr-mahn/eel bahr-tehn-dehr]
The bartender

Un drink
[oon drink]
A drink

Un succo di frutta
[oon soo-coh dee froot-tah]
A fruit drink

Una bibita
[oo-nah bee-bee-tah]
A soft drink

Una bottiglia di acqua minerale
[oo-nah boh-tee-lya dee ah-qwah mee-neh-rah-leh]
A bottle of mineral water

Un bicchiere di Negramaro
[oon bee-kee-eh-reh dee neh-grah-mah-roh]
A glass of Negramaro

della Birra (chiara, scura)
[dehl-lah beer-rah (kee-ah-rah, scoo-rah]
Some beer (light, dark)

del vino (rosso, bianco)
[dehl vee-noh (rohs-soh, bee-ahn-coh]
Some wine (red, white)

prendiamone un altro
[prehn-dee-ah-moh-neh oon ahl-troh]
let's have another

Salute!
[sah-loo-teh]
To your health!

Cin Cin!
[cheen cheen]
To your health!

Chapter 31: At the restaurant / Al ristorante

Dove si trova un buon ristorante?
[doh-veh see troh-vah oon bwon rees-toh-rahn-teh]
Where is there a good restaurant?

Mi può consigliare...?
[mee pwoh cohn-see-lyah-reh]
Can you recommend …?

un bar
[oon bahr]
a bar

un café
[oon cah-feh]
a café

un ristorante
[oon rees-toh-rahn-teh]
a restaurant

Vorrei ..., per favore
[voh-reh-ee…, pehr fah-voh-reh]
I'd like …, please

un tavolo per (cinque)
[oon tah-voh-loh pehr (cheen-qweh)]
a table for (five)

la sezione (non) fumatori
[lah seh-tsyoh-neh (nohn) foo-mah-toh-ree]
the (non)smoking section

Cosa consiglia?
[coh-sah cohn-see-lee-ah]
What would you recommend?

la lista delle bevande
[lah lees-tah deh-leh beh-vahn-deh]
the drink list

la carta dei vini
[lah cahr-tah deh-ee vee-nee]
the wine list

il menu
[eel meh-noo]
the menu

quel piatto
[qwel pee-aht-toh]
that dish

Colazione
[coh-lah-tsyoh-neh]
Breakfast

Pranzo
[prahn-tsoh]
Lunch

Cena
[cheh-nah]
Dinner

Cena
[cheh-nah]
Supper

Un panino
[oon pah-nee-noh]
A sandwich

Un tramezzino
[oon trah-meh-tsee-noh]
A tramezzino sandwich

Uno snack
[oo-noh snack]
A snack

A che ora viene servita la cena?
[ah keh oh-rah vee-eh-neh sehr-vee-tah lah cheh-nah]
At what time is dinner served?

Potremmo pranzare (cenare) adesso?
[poh-trehm-moh prahn-zah-reh (cheh-nah-reh) ah-dehs-soh]
Can we have lunch (dinner) now?

La cameriera
[lah cah-meh-ree-eh-rah]
The waitress

Il cameriere
[eel cah-meh-ree-eh-reh]
The waiter

Il maître
[eel meh-tr]
The headwaiter

Cameriere!
[cah-meh-ree-eh-reh]
Waiter!

Scusi?
[scoo-see]
excuse me! (to call waiter/waitress)

Siamo in due
[see-ah-moh een doo-eh]
There are two of us

Un tavolo vicino alla finestra, per favore
[oon tah-voh-loh vee-chee-noh ahl-lah fee-neh-strah, pehr fah-voh-reh]
Give me a table near the window

Per favore, mi può portare il menu?
[pehr fah-voh-reh, mee pwoh pohr-tah-reh eel meh-noo]
Please, bring me the menu

Vogliamo cenare à la carte
[voh-lee-ah-moh cheh-nah-reh ah lah cahrt]
We want to dine à la carte

Menu a prezzo fisso
[meh-noo ah preh-tsoh fees-soh]
fixed price menu

Tavolo
[tah-voh-loh]
Table

Una forchetta
[oo-nah fohr-ket-tah]
A fork

Un coltello
[oon cohl-tehl-loh]
A knife

Un piatto
[oon pee-ah-toh]
A plate

Un cucchiaino
[oon coo-kee-ah-ee-noh]
A teaspoon

Un cucchiaio
[oon coo-kee-ah-yoh]
A tablespoon

Un cucchiaio
[oon coo-kee-ah-yoh]
A spoon

La tazza
[lah tah-tsah]
the cup

Il bicchiere
[eel bee-kee-eh-reh]
the glass

tovagliolo
[toh-vah-lee-oh-loh]
napkin

Il piatto principale
[eel pee-ah-toh preen-chee-pah-leh]
the main course

Vorrei qualcosa di semplice
[voh-reh-ee quahl-coh-sah dee sehm-plee-cheh]
I want something simple

Non troppo piccante
[nohn trohp-poh pee-cahn-teh]
Not too spicy

Mi piace la carne al sangue
[mee pee-ah-cheh la cahr-neh ahl sahn-gweh]
I like the meat rare

ben cotta
[behn coht-tah]
Well done

da portare via, per favore
[dah pohr-tah-reh vee-ah, pehr fah-voh-reh]
Take it away, please

Questo è freddo
[qwes-toh eh freh-doh]
This is cold

Non ho ordinato questo
[nohn hoh ohr-dee-nah-toh qweh-stoh]
I did not order this

Posso cambiarlo con un'insalata?
[pohs-soh cahm-bee-ahr-loh cohn oon een-sah-lah-tah]
May i change this for a salad?

Il conto, per favore
[eel cohn-toh, pehr fah-voh-reh]
The check, please

Il conto
[eel cohn-toh]
The bill

lo scontrino
[loh scohn-tree-noh]
The receipt

Posso avere il conto, per favore?
[poh-soh ah-veh-reh eel cohn-toh, pehr fah-voh-reh]
could I have the bill, please?

il coperto è incluso?
[eel coh-pehr-toh eh een-cloo-soh]
Is the service charge included?

C'è un errore nel conto
[cheh oon ehr-roh-reh nehl cohn-toh]
There is a mistake in the bill

Questi addebiti a cosa si riferiscono?
[qweh-stee ah-deh-bee-tee ah coh-sah see ree-feh-rees-coh-noh]
What are these charges for?

Tenga il resto
[tehn-gah eel reh-stoh]
Keep the change

Il cibo e il servizio sono stati ottimi
[eel chee-boh eh eel sehr-vee-tsee-oh soh-noh stah-tee oh-tee-mee]
The food and service were excellent

Acqua potabile
[ah-qwah poh-tah-bee-leh]
Drinking water

con ghiaccio
[cohn gyee-ah-tchoh]
with ice

senza ghiaccio
[sehn-tsah gyee-ah-tchoh]
without ice

antipasto
[ahn-tee-pah-stoh]
starter

il dolce
[eel dohl-cheh]
the dessert

il pesce
[eel peh-sheh]
the fish

la carne
[lah cahr-neh]
the meat

l'insalata
[leen-sah-lah-tah]
the salad

la zuppa
[la zoop-pah]
the soup

pepe
[peh-peh]
pepper

sale
[sah-leh]
salt

zucchero
[zoo-ke-roh]
sugar

un altro..., per favore
[oon ahl-troh..., pehr fah-voh-reh]
another ..., please

Qual è la specialità locale?
[qwahl-eh lah speh-cha-lee-tah loh-cah-leh]
What's the local speciality?

Qual è il piatto della casa?
[qwahl-eh eel pyah-toh dehl-lah cah-sah]
What's the local speciality?

Cos'è quello?
[coh-seh qwel-loh]
What's that?

Chapter 32: Foods / Il cibo

Il pane
[eel pah-neh]
The bread

Il burro
[eel boor-roh]
The butter

Lo zucchero
[loh zook-keh-roh]
The sugar

Il sale
[eel sah-leh]
The salt

Il pepe
[eel peh-peh]
The pepper

La salsa
[lah sahl-sah]
The sauce

L'olio
[loh-leeh-oh]
The oil

L'aceto
[lah-cheh-toh]
The vinegar

La mostarda
[lah mohs-tahr-dah]
The mustard

L'aglio
[lah-lee-oh]
The garlic

del pollo arrosto
[dehl pohl-loh ah-roh-stoh]
Some roast chicken

del pollo fritto
[dehl pohl-loh freet-toh]
Some fried chicken

Manzo
[mahn-zoh]
beef

agnello
[ah-nee-yel-loh]
lamb

fegato
[feh-gah-toh]
liver

maiale
[mah-yah-leh]
pork

arrosto di manzo
[ahr-roh-stoh dee mahn-zoh]
roast beef

bistecca
[bees-tek-cah]
Steak

salsicce
[sahl-see-tcheh]
sausages

vitello
[vee-tehl-loh]
veal

orata
[oh-rah-tah]
sea bream

spigola
[spee-goh-lah]
sea bass

calamaro
[cah-lah-mah-roh]
squid

aragosta
[ah-rah-goh-stah]
lobster

sardine
[sahr-dee-neh]
sardines

gamberi
[gahm-beh-ree]
shrimps

polpo
[pohl-poh]
octopus

cozze
[coh-tseh]
mussels

Bruschetta
[broos-ket-tah]
Toasted bread topped with fresh diced tomatoes, garlic, basil, olive oil, salt.

Tagliere di affettati
[tah-lee-eh-reh dee ah-feht-tah-tee]
(assortment of cured meats)

Insalata Caprese
[een-sah-lah-tah cah-preh-seh]
Fresh slices of tomatoes, mozzarella, basil, olive oil, salt.

Grigliata di verdure
[gree-lyah-tah dee vehr-doo-reh]
(grilled mixed vegetables)

Pizza Margherita
[pee-tsah mahr-gwe-ree-tah]
(Tomato, mozzarella, olive oil and basil)

Rigatoni alla Amatriciana
[ree-gah-toh-nee ahl-lah-mah-tree-chah-nah]
(pasta with tomato sauce, pork cheek, pepper)

Rigatoni alla Carbonara
[ree-gah-toh-nee ahl-lah cahr-boh-nah-rah]
(pasta with pork cheek, creamy egg and pecorino cheese, pepper)

Spaghetti Cacio e Pepe
[spah-gweh-tee cah-tcho eh peh-peh]
(pasta with creamy pecorino cheese and pepper)

Tonnarelli alla Gricia
[tohn-nah-rehl-lee ahl-lah gree-cah]
(long pasta with pork cheek, creamy pecorino cheese, pepper)

Tiramisù
[tee-rah-mee-soo]
Dessert with layers of Savoiardi, mascarpone cream, espresso, liqueur, cocoa

Chapter 33: Menu breakfast foods / La colazione

Posso avere del succo di frutta, per favore?
[poh-tsoh ah-veh-reh dehl sooc-coh dee froot-tah, pehr fah-voh-reh]
May I have some fruit juice?

spremuta d'arancia
[spreh-moo-tah dah-rahn-cha]
orange juice

prugne cotte
[proo-nee-eh coh-teh]
stewed prunes

succo di pomodoro
[sooc-coh dee poh-moh-doh-roh]
tomato juice

marmellata
[mahr-mehl-lah-tah]
marmalade

toast con la marmellata
[tohs-t cohn lah mahr-mehl-lah-tah]
toast and jam

panini
[pah-nee-nee]
rolls

una omelette
[oo-nah ohm-leht]
an omelet

uova
[woh-vah]
eggs

Chapter 33: Menu breakfast foods / La colazione

uova alla coque
[woh-vah ahl-lah kok]
soft-boiled eggs

uova sode cottura media
[woh-vah soh-deh coht-too-rah meh-dee-ah]
medium boiled eggs

uova sode ben cotte
[woh-vah soh-deh behn coht-teh]
hard-boiled eggs

uova al tegamino
[woh-vah ahl teh-gah-mee-noh]
fried egg

uova strapazzate
[woh-vah strah-pah-tsah-teh]
scrambled eggs

uova e pancetta
[woh-vah eh pahn-tchet-tah]
bacon and eggs

uova e prosciutto
[woh-vah eh proh-shoot-toh]
ham and eggs

cappuccino
[cahp-poot-chee-noh]
cappuccino

latte
[laht-teh]
milk

caffé
[cah-feh]
coffee

tè
[teh]
tea

camomilla
[cah-moh-meel-lah]
chamomile

latte macchiato
[laht-teh mah-kee-ah-toh]
milk with coffee

caffelatte
[cah-feh-laht-teh]
white coffee

caffé lungo
[cah-feh loon-goh]
large coffee

cornetto
[cohr-net-toh]
croissant

biscotti
[bee-scott-tee]
cookies

fette biscottate
[feh-teh bees-coh-tah-teh]
rusks

avena
[ah-veh-nah]
oats

frutta
[froot-tah]
fruits

burro
[boor-roh]
butter

miele
[mee-eh-leh]
honey

cioccolata calda
[choc-coh-lah-tah cahl-dah]
hot chocolate

frullato
[froo-lah-toh]
shake

frappé
[frah-peh]
milk shake

torta
[tohr-tah]
cake

una fetta di torta
[oo-nah feht-tah dee tohr-tah]
a slice of cake

Chapter 34: Special Diets & Allergies / Dieta e Allergie

C'è un ristorante vegetariano qui vicino?
[cheh oon rees-toh-rahn-teh veh-djeh-tah-ree-ah-noh qwee vee-chee-noh]
Is there a vegetarian restaurant near here?

Avete dei piatti vegetariani?
[ah-veh-teh deh-ee pyat-tee veh-djeh-tah-ree-ah-nee]
Do you have vegetarian food?

Potrebbe preparare un/uno/una .... senza ...
[poh-treh-beh preh-pah-rah-reh oon/oo-noh/oo-nah... sehn-tsah]
Could you prepare a ... without ...?

brodo di carne
[broh-doh dee cahr-neh]
meat stock

Sono allergico/allergica (m/f)
[soh-noh ahl-lehr-jee-coh/ahl-lehr-jee-cah]
I'm allergic ...

ai latticini
[ah-ee laht-tee-chee-nee]
to dairy products

al glutine
[ahl gloo-tee-neh]
to gluten

al glutammato
[ahl gloo-tah-mah-toh]
to MSG

alla frutta secca
[ahl-lah froot-tah seh-cah]
to nuts

ai frutti di mare
[ah-ee froot-tee dee mah-reh]
to seafood

Sedano
[seh-dah-noh]
celery

Chapter 35: Appetizer, soups and entrées / Antipasti, Zuppe, primi piatti

Antipasto
[ahn-tee-pah-stoh]
Appetizer

Antipasto di mare
[ahn-tee-pah-stoh dee mah-reh]
seafood appetizer

salumi
[sah-loo-mee]
cured meat

formaggi
[fohr-mah-djee]
cheeses

noccioline
[noh-tcho-lee-neh]
peanuts

patatine
[pah-tah-tee-neh]
chips

Vorrei una zuppa di pollo
[voh-reh-ee oo-nah zoop-pah dee pohl-loh]
I want some chicken soup

minestrone
[mee-neh-stroh-neh]
vegetable soup

zuppa di legumi
[zoop-pah dee leh-goo-mee]
legumes soup

lenticchie
[lehn-tee-kee-eh]
lentils

ceci
[che-tchee]
chickpeas

fagioli
[fah-djoh-lee]
beans

riso
[ree-soh]
rice

farro
[fahr-roh]
spelled

ravioli
[rah-vee-oh-lee]
Italian dumplings

pasta con...
[pah-stah cohn]
pasta with...

sugo
[soo-goh]
tomato sauce

pesto
[peh-stoh]
pesto

ragù alla bolognese
[rah-goo ahl-lah boh-loh-nee-eh-seh]
Bolognese sauce

in bianco
[een bee-ahn-coh]
butter or oil

lasagna
[lah-sah-nyah]
lasagna

pasta al forno
[pah-stah ahl fohr-noh]
baked pasta

Chapter 36: Vegetables and salad / Verdure e insalata

Vorrei degli asparagi
[voh-reh-ee deh-lee ah-spah-rah-djee]
I want some asparagus

carote
[cah-roh-teh]
carrots

cavolo
[cah-voh-loh]
cabbage

cavolfiore
[cah-vohl-fyoh-reh]
cauliflower

sedano
[seh-dah-noh]
celery

olive
[oh-lee-veh]
olives

prezzemolo
[preh-tseh-moh-loh]
parsley

origano
[oh-ree-gah-noh]
oregano

alloro
[ahl-loh-roh]
bay tree

cetriolo
[che-tree-oh-loh]
cucumber

menta
[mehn-tah]
mint

basilico
[bah-see-lee-coh]
basil

insalata
[een-sah-lah-tah]
salad

lattuga
[lah-too-gah]
letuce

valeriana
[vah-leh-ryah-nah]
valerian

rucola
[roo-coh-lah]
arugula/ rocket

funghi
[foon-gyee]
mushrooms

cipolle
[chee-poll-leh]
onions

piselli
[pee-seh-lee]
peas

peperoni
[peh-peh-roh-nee]
peppers

spinaci
[spee-nah-chee]
spinach

patate
[pah-tah-teh]
potatoes

patate lesse
[pah-tah-teh lehs-seh]
boiled potatoes

patatine fritte
[pah-tah-tee-neh freet-teh]
fried potatoes

puré di patate
[poo-reh dee pah-tah-teh]
mashed potatoes

pomodori
[poh-moh-doh-ree]
tomatoes

zucca
[zooc-cah]
pumpkin

melanzane
[meh-lahn-tsah-neh]
eggplant

zucchine
[zoo-kee-neh]
zucchinis

aglio
[ah-lee-oh]
garlic

rosmarino
[rohs-mah-ree-noh]
rosemary

carciofi
[cahr-tchoh-fee]
artichokes

rapa
[rah-pah]
turnip

cicoria
[chee-coh-ree-ah]
chicory

bietola
[bee-eh-toh-lah]
chard

cardo
[cahr-doh]
cardoon

Chapter 37: Fruits – Frutta

Vorrei una mela
[voh-reh-ee oo-nah meh-lah]
I want an apple

Pera
[peh-rah]
pear

delle ciliegie
[dehl-leh chee-lee-eh-djeh]
some cherries

un pompelmo
[oon pawn-pehl-moh]
a grapefruit

un'arancia
[oon ah-rahn-tcha]
an orange

dell'uva
[dehl oo-vah]
some grapes

limone
[lee-moh-neh]
lemon

melone
[meh-loh-neh]
melon

anguria
[ahn-goo-ryah]
watermelon

pesca
[peh-scah]
peach

lamponi
[lahm-poh-nee]
raspberries

fragole
[frah-goh-leh]
strawberries

more
[moh-reh]
blackberries

ribes
[ree-bes]
currant

albicocca
[ahl-bee-cohc-cah]
apricot

ananas
[ah-nah-nahs]
pineapple

banana
[bah-nah-nah]
banana

kiwi
[kee-wee]
kiwi

mandarino
[mahn-dah-ree-noh]
Tangerine

Chapter 38: Beverages & Drinks / Bevande

Caffé lungo
[cah-feh loon-goh]
some black coffee

Caffé
[cah-feh]
espresso

un caffé
[oon cah-feh]
(cup of) coffee …

Caffé con panna
[cah-feh cohn pahn-nah]
Coffee with cream

Caffé con panna
[cah-feh cohn pahn-nah]
coffee with whipped cream

decaffeinato
[deh-cah-feh-ee-nah-toh]
decaffeinated

caffelatte
[cah-feh-laht-teh]
white coffee

caffé freddo
[cah-feh frehd-doh]
iced coffee

caffé solubile
[cah-feh soh-loo-bee-leh]
instant coffee

del latte
[dehl laht-teh]
some milk

del tè
[dehl teh]
some tea

un tè
[oon teh]
(cup of) tea ...

tè con latte
[teh cohn laht-teh]
tea with milk

infuso
[een-foo-soh]
herb tea

tè alla menta
[teh ahl-lah mehn-tah]
mint tea

tè al limone
[teh ahl lee-moh-neh]
lemon tea

birra
[beer-rah]
beer

birra alla spina
[beer-rah ahl-lah spee-nah]
draught beer

birra scura
[beer-rah scoo-rah]
dark beer

birra rossa
[beer-rah rohs-sah]
fairly dark beer

la bottiglia
[lah boht-tee-lyah]
the bottle

gin
[geen]
gin

acqua
[ac-qwah]
water

calda
[cahl-dah]
hot

acqua minerale
[ac-qwah mee-neh-rah-leh]
mineral water

acqua frizzante
[ac-qwah free-tsahn-teh]
sparkling mineral water

frizzante
[free-tsahn-teh]
Fizzy

succo d'arancia
[sooc-coh dah-rahn-tcha]
orange juice

spremuta d'arancia
[spreh-moo-tah dah-rahn-tcha]
fresh orange juice

limonata
[lee-moh-nah-tah]
lemonade

vino
[vee-noh]
wine

vino rosso
[vee-noh ross-oh]
red wine

vino bianco
[vee-noh bee-ahn-coh]
white wine

rosé
[raw-zey]
rosé

carta dei vini
[cahr-tah deh-ee vee-nee]
wine list

vino della casa
[vee-noh dehl-lah cah-sah]
regional wine

analcolico
[ahn-ahl-coh-lee-coh]
soft drink

zucchero
[zooc-keh-roh]
sugar

senza zucchero
[sehn-tsah zooc-keh-roh]
without sugar

alcool
[ahl-coh-ohl]
alcohol

brut
[broot]
very dry

a temperatura ambiente
[ah tehm-peh-rah-too-rah ahm-bee-ehn-teh]
at room temperature

ghiaccio
[gwee-at-choh]
ice

cubetto di ghiaccio
[coo-bet-toh dee gwee-at-choh]
ice cube

digestivo
[dee-jess-tee-voh]
liqueur

Chapter 39: Desserts – Les desserts

Potrei avere un po' di torta?
[poh-treh-ee ah-veh-reh oon poh dee tohr-tah]
May I have some cake?

del formaggio
[dehl fohr-mah-djoh]
some cheese

dei biscotti
[deh-ee bee-scott-tee]
some cookies

delle crêpes
[dehl-leh creh-pp]
some crêpes

della crema pasticcera
[dehl-lah creh-mah pah-stee-tcheh-rah]
some custard

gelato
[djeh-lah-toh]
ice cream

del gelato al cioccolato
[dehl djeh-lah-toh ahl tchoh-coh-lah-toh]
some chocolate ice cream

Chapter 40: Bar / café

caffelatte con schiuma
[cah-feh-lah-teh cohn skee-oo-mah]
white creamy coffee

caffelatte con schiuma in tazza grande
[cah-feh-lah-teh cohn skee-oo-mah een tah-tsah grahn-deh]
large white creamy coffee

Un caffè
[oon cah-feh]
a coffee

Un caffè macchiato caldo
[oon cah-feh mah-kyah-toh cahl-doh]
coffee with hot milk

Un caffè macchiato freddo
[oon cah-feh mah-kyah-toh freh-doh]
coffee with cold milk

un'aranciata
[oon ah-rahn-cha-tah]
an orangeade

con limone
[cohn lee-moh-neh]
with lemon

senza zucchero
[sehn-tsah zoo-keh-roh]
no sugar

per due
[pehr doo-eh]
for two

per me
[pehr meh]
for me

per lui/lei
[pehr loo-ee/leh-ee]
for him/her

per noi
[pehr noh-ee]
for us

con ghiaccio, per favore
[cohn gwee-ah-tcho, pehr fah-voh-reh]
with ice, please

dell'acqua minerale
[dehl-lah-qwah mee-neh-rah-leh]
some mineral water

effervescente
[eh-fehr-veh-shehn-teh]
sparkling

liscia
[lee-sha]
still

Chapter 41: Reading the menu – Leggere il menu

In Italy, you are not obliged to leave tips in restaurants (it's optional), but everyone pays a cover charge that includes table service and bread.

Piatto del giorno 7,50 €: pesce o Carne o Pollo con verdure e patatine fritte
[pee-ah-toh dehl djohr-noh 7,50€: peh-sheh oh cahr-neh cohn vehr-doo-reh eh pah-tah-tee-neh freet-teh]
Dish of the day 7 € 50 – fish or meat or poultry with veg and French fries.

Menu pranzo: antipasto + primo + caffè
[meh-noo prahn-tsoh: ahn-tee-pah-stoh + pree-moh + cah-feh]
Lunchtime menu – starter + main course + coffee.

Coperto
[coh-pehr-toh]
cover, service

Chapter 42: In a restaurant – In un ristorante

Cosa prende?
[coh-sah prehn-deh]
What will you have?

Un tè con latte, per favore
[oon teh cohn laht-teh, pehr fah-voh-reh]
A tea with milk, please

Vorrei prenotare un tavolo per ... persone
[vohr-reh-ee preh-noh-tah-reh oon tah-voh-loh pehr... pehr-soh-neh]
I'd like to book a table for ... people

Per stasera/domani sera/per le sette e trenta
[pehr stah-seh-rah/doh-mah-nee/pehr leh seht-teh e trehn-tah]
For tonight/for tomorrow night/for 7.30

Un tavolo per due?
[oon tah-voh-loh pehr doo-eh]
A table for two?

Può portarci il menu, per favore?
[pwoh pohr-tahr-chee eel meh-noo, pehr fah-voh-reh]
The menu, please

Qual è il piatto del giorno?
[qwah-leh eel pyat-toh dehl djohr-noh]
What is the dish of the day?

Prendo il menu a ... euro, per favore
[prehn-doh eel meh-noo ah... eh-oo-roh, pehr fah-voh-reh]
I'll have the menu at ... euros, please

Può consigliarmi un piatto locale?
[pwoh cohn-see-lyahr-mee oon pyah-toh loh-cah-leh]
Can you recommend a local dish?

Cosa c'è dentro?
[coh-sah cheh dehn-troh]
What is in this?

Prendo questo
[prehn-doh qweh-stoh]
I'll have this

dell'altro pane...
[dehl-lahl-troh pah-neh]
More bread...

dell'altra acqua...
[dehl-lahl-trah ah-qwah]
More water...

per favore
[pehr fah-voh-reh]
please

il conto, per favore
[eel cohn-toh, pehr fah-voh-reh]
The bill, please

Il servizio è incluso?
[eel sehr-vee-tsyoh eh een-cloo-soh]
Is service included?

Chapter 43: Vegetarian / Vegetariano

Ci sono ristoranti vegetariani qui?
[chee soh-noh rees-toh-tahn-tee veh-djeh-tah-ree-ah-nee qwee]
Are there any vegetarian restaurants here?

Avete dei piatti vegetariani?
[ah-veh-teh deh-ee pyat-tee veh-djeh-tah-ree-ah-nee]
Do you have any vegetarian dishes?

Quali sono i piatti senza carne/pesce?
[qwah-lee soh-noh ee pyat-tee sehn-tsah cahr-neh/peh-sheh]
Which dishes have no meat/fish?

Vorrei la pasta come primo piatto
[voh-reh-ee lah pah-stah coh-meh pree-moh pee-aht-toh]
I'd like pasta as a main course

Non mi piace la carne
[nohn mee pee-ah-cheh lah cahr-neh]
I don't like meat

è fatto con brodo vegetale?
[eh faht-toh cohn broh-doh veh-djeh-tah-leh]
Is it made with vegetable stock?

Chapter 44: Wines and spirits / Vino e alcolici

La carta dei vini, per favore
[lah cahr-tah deh-ee vee-nee, pehr fah-voh-reh]
The wine list, please

vino bianco/vino rosso
[vee-noh bee-ahn-coh/vee-noh rohs-soh]
white wine/red wine

Può consigliarci un buon vino?
[pwoh cohn-see-lee-ahr-chee oon bwohn vee-noh]
Can you recommend a good wine?

Una bottiglia..
[oo-nah boh-tee-lyah]
A bottle…

Una caraffa
[oo-nah cah-rahf-fah]
A carafe…

del vino della casa
[dehl vee-noh dehl-lah cah-sah]
of the house wine

Quali liquori avete?
[qwah-lee lee-qwoh-ree ah-veh-teh]
What liqueurs do you have?

Part 6: Traveling & Planning (Trips, Weather, Activities) – Viaggi e pianificazione (meteo e attività)

Learning Italian often inspires you to daydream about traveling and planning trips to Italian-speaking countries. This type of wanderlust can be greatly expedited with some Italian vocabulary and phrases related to traveling and planning. From the beach to the mountains, from camping to sightseeing, this chapter will give you some practical and useful hints for planning your dream holiday.

Chapter 45: Accomodations – Alloggi

un hotel economico
[oon hotel eh-coh-noh-mee-coh]
an inexpensive hotel

sto cercando un buon hotel
[stoh chehr-chan-doh oon boo-ohn hotel]
I am looking for a good hotel

una pensione
[oo-nah pen-see-oh-neh]
a boarding house

appartamento completamente arredato
[ahp-pahr-tah-mehn-toh cohm-pleh-tah-mehn-teh ah-reh-dah-toh]
full furnished apartment

(non) voglio stare in centro
[(nohn) voh-lee-oh stah-reh een chen-troh]
I (do not) want to be at the center of town

dove non c'è rumore
[doh-veh nohn cheh roo-moh-reh]
where it is not noisy

Vorrei prenotare una stanza, per favore
[voh-reh-ee preh-noh-tah-reh oo-nah stahn-tsah, pehr fah-voh-reh]
I'd like to book a room, please.

Ho una prenotazione per oggi
[hoh oo-nah preh-noh-tah-tsyoh-neh pehr odd-djee]
I have a reservation for today

il mio nome è
[eel mee-oh noh-meh eh]
My name is

Chapter 45: Accomodations – Alloggi

Avete una stanza, un posto libero?
[ah-veh-teh oo-nah stahn-tsah, oon poh-stoh lee-beh-roh]
Do you have a room, a vacancy?

una stanza con aria condizionata
[oo-nah stahn-tsah cohn ah-ree-ah cohn-dee-tsyoh-nah-tah]
an air conditioned room

una singola
[oo-nah seen-goh-lah]
A single room

una doppia
[oo-nah doh-pyah]
A double room

una doppia
[oo-nah doh-pyah]
twin room

senza pasti/ senza vitto
[sehn-tsah pah-stee/sehn-tsah veet-toh]
without meals

con un letto matrimoniale
[cohn oon leht-toh mah-tree-moh-nee-ah-leh]
with a double bed

con bagno
[cohn bah-nee-oh]
with a bathroom

con doccia
[cohn-doh-tchah]
with a shower

con due letti singoli
[cohn doo-eh leht-tee seen-goh-lee]
with twin beds

una suite
[oo-nah sweet]
a suite

per questa notte
[pehr qweh-stah not-teh]
for tonight

per tre giorni
[pehr treh djohr-nee]
for three days

Vorrei restare per (due) notti
[vohr-reh-ee reh-stah-reh pehr (doo-eh) not-tee]
I'd like to stay for (two) nights

per due persone
[pehr doo-eh pehr-soh-neh]
for two

Qual è il costo a notte?
[qwah-leh eel coh-stoh ah not-teh]
What is the rate per day?

Quanto costa a...?
[qwahn-toh coh-stah ah]
How much is it per …?

notte
[not-teh]
night

persona
[pehr-soh-nah]
person

Tasse e servizio in camera sono inclusi?
[tahs-seh eh sehr-vee-tsyoh een cah-meh-rah soh-noh een-cloo-see]
Are tax and room service included?

Vorrei vedere la stanza
[vohr-reh-ee veh-deh-reh lah stahn-tsah]
I would like to see the room

Non mi piace questa
[nohn mee pyah-tcheh qweh-stah]
I do not like this one

al piano di sopra
[ahl pyah-noh dee soh-prah]
upstairs

al piano di sotto
[ahl pyah-noh dee soht-toh]
downstairs

c'è l'ascensore?
[cheh lah-shehn-soh-reh]
Is there an elevator?

una cassaforte
[oo-nah cahs-sah-fohr-teh]
a safe

il servizio in camera, per favore
[eel sehr-vee-tsyoh een cah-meh-rah, pehr fah-voh-reh]
Room service, please

Per favore, può mandare un facchino nella mia stanza?
[pehr fah-voh-reh, pwoh mahn-dah-reh oon fah-kee-noh nehl-lah mee-ah stahn-tsah]
Please send a porter to my room

Una cameriera
[oo-nah cah-meh-ryeh-rah]
A chambermaid

Un fattorino
[oon faht-toh-ree-noh]
A bellhop

Per favore, mi chiami alle 9
[pehr fah-voh-reh, mee kee-ah-mee ahl-leh noh-veh]
Please call me at nine o'clock

Vorrei la colazione in stanza
[voh-reh-ee lah coh-lah-tsyoh-neh een stahn-tsah]
I want breakfast in my room

Torni più tardi
[tohr-nee pyoo tahr-dee]
Come back later

Può portarmi un'altra coperta?
[pwoh pohr-tahr-mee oon ahl-trah coh-pehr-tah]
Bring me another blanket

Potrei avere un'altra (coperta)?
[poh-treh-ee ah-veh-reh oon ahl-trah (coh-pehr-tah)]
Can I get another (blanket)?

Un cuscino
[oon coo-shee-noh]
A pillow

Una federa
[oo-nah feh-deh-rah]
A pillowcase

lenzuolo
[lehn-tswoh-loh]
sheet

appendiabiti
[ah-pehn-dee-ah-bee-tee]
hangers

sapone
[sah-poh-neh]
soap

Asciugamani
[ah-shoo-gah-mah-nee]
Towels

un tappetino per il bagno
[oon tah-peh-tee-noh pehr eel bah-nyoh]
a bath mat

la vasca da bagno
[lah vahs-cah dah bah-nyoh]
the bathtub

il lavabo
[eel lah-vah-boh]
the sink

la carta igienica
[lah cahr-tah ee-djeh-nee-cah]
toilet paper

Vorrei parlare con il direttore
[vohr-reh-ee pahr-lah-reh cohn eel dee-reht-toh-reh]
I would like to speak to the manager

La mia chiave, per favore
[lah mee-ah kee-ah-veh, pehr fah-voh-reh]
My room key, please

Potrei avere la mia chiave, per favore?
[pot-reh-ee ah-veh-reh lah mee-ah kee-ah-veh, pehr fah-voh-reh]
Could I have my key, please?

Ci sono lettere o messaggi per me?
[chee soh-noh leht-teh-reh oh mess-sah-djee pehr meh]
Have I any letters or messages?

Qual è il numero della mia stanza?
[qwah-leh eel noo-meh-roh dehl-lah mee-ah stahn-tsah]
What is my room number?

Vado via alle 10.
[vah-doh vee-ah ahl-leh dee-eh-tchee]
I am leaving at ten o'clock

per favore, mi faccia il conto
[pehr fah-voh-reh, mee fah-tcha eel cohn-toh]
Please make out my bill

Accetta un assegno?
[ah-tcheh-tah oon ahs-seh-nyoh]
Will you accept a check?

Posso pagare con la carta di credito?
[pohs-soh pah-gah-reh cohn lah cahr-tah dee creh-dee-toh]
Can I pay by credit card?

Per favore, può inviare la mia lettera a...
[pehr fah-voh-reh, pwoh een-vee-ah-reh lah mee-ah let-teh-rah ah]
Please forward my mail to

Posso lasciare i bagagli qui fino a domani?
[pohs-soh lah-shah-reh ee bah-gal-lee qwee fee-noh ah doh-mah-nee]
May I store baggage here until tomorrow?

Dov'è un...?
[doh-veh oon]
Where's a ...?

campeggio
[cahm-peh-djoh]
camping ground

ostello
[oh-stehl-loh]
youth hostel

può consigliarmi un posto...?
[pwoh cohn-see-lee-ahr-mee oon poh-stoh]
Can you recommend somewhere...?

economico
[eh-coh-noh-mee-coh]
cheap

buono
[bwoh-noh]
good

vicino
[vee-chee-noh]
nearby

Posso campeggiare qui?
[pohs-soh cahm-peh-djah-reh qwee]
Am I allowed to camp here?

dov'è il campeggio più vicino?
[doh-veh eel cahm-peh-djoh pyoo vee-chee-noh]
Where's the nearest camp site?

A che ora viene servita la colazione?
[ah keh oh-rah vyeh-neh sehr-vee-tah lah coh-lah-tsyoh-neh]
When/Where is breakfast served?

Per favore, mi svegli alle (sette)
[pehr fah-voh-reh, mee sveh-lee ahl-leh (seht-teh)]
Please wake me at (seven)

La stanza è...
[lah stahn-tsah eh]
The room is too ...

costosa
[coh-stoh-sah]
expensive

rumorosa
[roo-moh-roh-sah]
noisy

piccola
[pee-coh-lah]
small

non funziona...
[nohn foon-tsyoh-nah]
doesn't work...

l'aria condizionata
[lah-ree-ah cohn-dee-tsyoh-nah-tah]
the air conditioning

il ventilatore
[eel vehn-tee-lah-toh-reh]
fan

il bagno non è pulito
[eel bah-nee-oh nohn eh poo-lee-toh]
the toilet isn't clean

A che ora è il checkout?
[ah keh oh-rah eh eel checkout]
What time is checkout?

Per favore, posso avere...?
[pehr fah-voh-reh, pohs-soh ah-veh-reh]
Could I have my..., please?

la mia cauzione
[lah mee-ah cah-oo-tsyoh-neh]
deposit

passaporto
[pahs-sah-pohr-toh]
passport

i miei valori
[ee mee-eh-ee vah-loh-ree]
valuables

Chapter 46: Weather – Il meteo

Che tempo fa?
[keh tehm-poh fah]
What's the weather like?

è nuovoloso
[eh noo-voh-loh-soh]
It's ...cloudy

fa freddo
[fah freh-doh]
It's ...cold

fa caldo
[fah cahl-doh]
It's ...hot

fa caldo
[fah cahl-doh]
It's ...warm

sta piovendo
[stah pyoh-vehn-doh]
It's ...raining

sta nevicando
[stah neh-vee-cahn-doh]
It's ...snowing

è soleggiato
[eh soh-leh-djah-toh]
It's ...sunny

c'è vento
[cheh vehn-toh]
It's ...windy

c'è nebbia
[cheh neh-byah]
It's...foggy

Chapter 47: Sightseeing – Giro turistico

Vorrei una guida che parli inglese
[voh-reh-ee oo-nah gwee-dah keh pahr-lee een-gleh-seh]
I want a guide who speaks English

qual è il costo orario (giornaliero)?
[qwah-leh eel coh-stoh oh-rah-ryoh (djohr-nah-lee-eh-roh)]
What is the charge per hour (day)?

Sono interessato alla pittura
[soh-noh een-teh-rehs-sah-toh ahl-lah peet-too-rah]
I am interested in painting

scultura
[scool-too-rah]
Sculpture

Architettura
[ahr-kee-teh-too-rah]
Architecture

il castello
[eel cahs-tell-loh]
The castle

la cattedrale
[lah cah-teh-drah-leh]
The cathedral

la chiesa
[lah kee-eh-sah]
church

Il museo
[eel moo-seh-oh]
The museum

Chapter 47: Sightseeing – Giro turistico

il monastero
[eel moh-nah-steh-roh]
monastery

il monumento
[eel moh-noo-mehn-toh]
monument

il centro storico
[eel chen-troh stoh-ree-coh]
old city

il palazzo
[eel pah-lah-tsoh]
palace

le rovine
[leh roh-veeh-neh]
ruins

lo stadio
[loh stah-dee-oh]
stadium

le statue
[leh stah-too-eh]
statues

la piazza centrale
[lah pee-ah-tsah chen-trah-leh]
main square

Dov'è l'entrata/uscita?
[doh-veh lehn-trah-tah/oo-shee-tah]
Where is the entrance/exit?

Quanto costa l'ingresso?
[qwahn-toh coh-stah leen-grehs-soh]
What is the price of admission?

C'è una riduzione per i bambini/gli studenti?
[cheh oo-nah ree-doo-tsyoh-neh pehr ee bahm-bee-nee/lee stoo-dehn-tee]
Is there a discount for children/students?

A che ora...?
[ah keh oh-rah]
What time does it …?

chiude
[kyoo-deh]
close

apre
[ah-preh]
open

Vorrei...
[voh-reh-ee]
I'd like …

un catalogo
[oon cah-tah-loh-goh]
a catalogue

una guida
[oo-nah-gwee-dah]
a guide

una cartina
[oo-nah cahr-tee-nah]
a local map

vorrei vedere...
[vohr-reh-ee veh-deh-reh]
I'd like to see …

Cos'è quello?
[coh-seh qwehl-loh]
What's that?

Posso fare delle foto?
[poh-soh fah-reh dehl-leh foh-toh]
Can I take photos?

Quando c'è il prossimo...?
[qwahn-doh cheh eel prohs-see-moh]
When's the next ...?

giro/ visita
[gee-roh/vee-see-tah]
tour

l'escursione giornaliera
[leh-scoor-see-oh-neh djohr-nah-lee-eh-rah]
day trip excursion

è incluso l'alloggio?
[eh een-cloo-soh lahl-loh-djoh]
Is the accomodation included?

il biglietto di ingresso
[eel bee-lee-eh-toh deen-grehs-soh]
the admission charge

il cibo
[eel chee-boh]
food

il trasporto
[eel trahs-pohr-toh]
transport

Quanto dura la visita?
[qwahn-toh doo-rah lah vee-see-tah]
How long is the tour?

A che ora dovremmo tornare?
[ah keh oh-rah doh-vrehm-moh tohr-nah-reh]
What time should we be back?

Chapter 48: Amusements – Divertimenti

Vorrei andare a un concerto
[voh-reh-ee ahn-dah-reh ah oon cohn-chehr-toh]
I would like to go to a concert

vorrei andare...
[voh-reh-ee ahn-dah-reh]
I feel like going ...

al cinema
[ahl chee-neh-mah]
To the movies

in un night club
[een oon night club]
To a night club

all'opera
[ahl oh-peh-rah]
To the opera

all'ufficio prenotazioni
[ahl oof-fee-choh preh-noh-tah-tsyoh-nee]
To the booking office

a teatro
[ah teh-ah-troh]
To the theatre

al ristorante
[ahl rees-toh-rahn-teh]
to the restaurant

A che ora inizia lo spettacolo serale/ il prossimo spettacolo?
[ah keh oh-rah ee-nee-tsyah loh speh-tah-coh-loh seh-rah-leh/ eel proh-see-moh speh-tah-coh-loh]
When does the evening performance, the futur show start?

Ci sono posti per questa sera?
[chee soh-noh poh-stee pehr qweh-stah seh-rah]
Have you any seats for tonight?

un posto prenotato/riservato
[oon poh-stoh preh-noh-tah-toh/ree-sehr-vah-toh]
A reserved seat

sulla balconata
[sool-lah bahl-coh-nah-tah]
In the balcony

Si vede bene da lì?
[see veh-deh beh-neh dah-lee]
Can I see well from there?

Dove possiamo andare a ballare?
[doh-veh pohs-see-ah-moh ahn-dah-reh ah bahl-lah-reh]
Where can we go to dance?

Mi concede questo ballo?
[mee cohn-cheh-deh qweh-stoh bahl-loh]
May I have this dance?

dove posso trovare...?
[doh-veh pohs-soh troh-vah-reh]
Where can I find…?

club
[club]
clubs

locali gay
[loh-cah-lee gay]
gay venues

pub
[pub]
pubs

Ti piace...?
[tee pyah-cheh]
Do you like …?

mi piace...
[mee pyah-cheh]
I like...

non mi piace...
[nohn mee pyah-cheh]
I don't like …

l'arte
[lahr-teh]
art

cucinare
[coo-chee-nah-reh]
cooking

i film
[ee feelm]
movies

i nightclub
[ee nightclub]
nightclubs

leggere
[leh-djeh-reh]
reading

fare shopping
[fah-reh shopping]
shopping

lo sport
[loh sport]
sport

viaggiare
[viah-djah-reh]
travelling

ballare
[bahl-lah-reh]
to dance

andare ai concerti
[ahn-dah-reh ah-ee cohn-chehr-tee]
go to concerts

ascoltare musica
[ah-scohl-tah-reh moo-see-cah]
listen to music

Chapter 49: Disabled travelers / Viaggiatori disabili

Quali servizi avete per persone disabili?
[qwah-lee sehr-vee-tsee ah-veh-teh pehr pehr-soh-neh dee-sah-bee-lee]
What facilities do you have for disabled people?

Ci sono bagni per disabili?
[chee soh-noh bah-nee pehr dee-sah-bee-lee]
Are there any toilets for the disabled?

Avete camere da letto al piano terra?
[ah-veh-teh cah-meh-reh dah leht-toh ahl pyah-noh tehr-rah]
Do you have any bedrooms on the ground floor?

C'è l'ascensore?
[cheh lah-shehn-soh-reh]
Is there a lift?

Dov'è l'ascensore?
[doh-veh lah-shehn-soh-reh]
Where is the lift?

Avete sedie a rotelle?
[ah-veh-teh seh-dee-eh ah roh-tehl-leh]
Do you have wheelchairs?

Si può visitare... in sedia a rotelle?
[see pwoh vee-see-tah-reh... een seh-dee-ah ah-roh-tehl-leh]
Can you visit … in a wheelchair?

Avete un ciclo di induzione?
[ah-veh-teh oon chee-cloh dee een-doo-tsyoh-neh]
Do you have an induction loop?

Ci sono sconti per le persone disabili?
[chee soh-noh scohn-tee pehr leh pehr-soh-neh dee-sah-bee-lee]
Is there a reduction for disabled people?

C'è un posto dove posso sedermi?
[cheh oon poh-stoh doh-veh pohs-soh seh-dehr-mee]
Is there somewhere I can sit down?

Chapter 50: With kids – Con i bambini

Un biglietto per un bambino
[oon bee-lee-eh-toh pehr oon bahm-bee-noh]
A child's ticket

Lui/lei ha... anni
[loo-ee/leh-ee ah… ahn-nee]
He/She is … years old

C'è uno sconto per i bambini?
[cheh oo-noh scohn-toh pehr ee bahm-bee-nee]
Is there a reduction for children?

Avete un menu per bambini?
[ah-veh-teh oon meh-noo pehr bahm-bee-nee]
Do you have a children's menu?

Si possono portare i bambini?
[see-pohs-soh-noh pohr-tah-reh ee bahm-bee-nee]
Is it OK to take children?

Avete...?
[ah-veh-teh]
Do you have…?

un seggiolone
[oon seh-djoh-loh-neh]
a high chair

una culla
[oo-nah cool-lah]
a cot

ho due figli
[hoh doo-eh fee-lee]
I have two children

lei ha figli?
[leh-ee hah fee-lee]
Do you have any children?

Part 7 : Money & Shopping – Soldi e acquisti

Whether you like saving money or blowing it before it even reaches your wallet, financial matters are a core part of everyday life. Having the ability to talk about money and a good understanding of monetary terms in Italian will be highly useful when using your Italian in real-life scenarios. If you are traveling in an Italian-speaking country, you will at some point need to ask how much something costs or have other such questions related to financial expenses.

Chapter 51: Money / Soldi

sportello bancomat
[spohr-tehl-loh bahn-coh-maht]
cash dispenser

prelievo contanti
[preh-lee-eh-voh cohn-tahn-tee]
cash withdrawal

Dove posso cambiare delle banconote?
[doh-veh pohs-soh cahm-bee-ah-reh dehl-leh bahn-coh-noh-teh]
Where can I change some money?

Quando apre la banca?
[qwahn-doh ah-preh lah bahn-cah]
When does the bank open?

Quando chiude la banca?
[qwahn-doh kyoo-deh lah bahn-cah]
When does the bank close?

Posso pagare in sterline/euro?
[pohs-soh pah-gah-reh een stehr-lee-neh/e-oo-roh]
Can I pay with pounds/euros?

Posso usare la mia carta in questo bancomat?
[pohs-soh oo-sah-reh lah mee-ah car-tah een qweh-stoh bahn-coh-maht]
Can I use my credit card with this cash dispenser?

Ha da cambiare?
[hah dah cahm-byah-reh]
Do you have any change?

Chapter 52: Banking / La banca

Dov'è la banca più vicina?
[doh-veh lah bahn-cah pyoo vee-chee-nah]
Where is the nearest bank?

A quale sportello posso incassare questo?
[ah qwah-leh spohr-tehl-loh pohs-soh een-cahs-sah-reh qweh-stoh]
At which window can I cash this?

Può cambiarlo per me?
[pwoh cahm-bee-ahr-loh pehr meh]
Can you change this for me?

incasserai l'assegno?
[een-cahs-seh-rah-ee lahs-seh-nyoh]
Will you cash a check?

Non mi dia pezzi troppo grossi
[nohn mee dee-ah peh-tsee trohp-poh gross-see]
Do not give me large bills

Potrei cambiare?
[poh-treh-ee cahm-bee-ah-reh]
May I have some change?

Una lettera di credito
[oo-nah let-teh-rah dee creh-dee-toh]
A letter of credit

un bonifico bancario
[oon boh-nee-fee-coh bahn-cah-ree-oh]
A bank draft

Qual è il tasso di cambio per il dollaro?
[qwah-leh eel tahs-soh dee cahm-bee oh pehr eel dohl-lah-roh]
What is the exchange rate on the dollar?

Dov'è...?
[doh-veh]
Where's …?

l'ATM
[lah-tee-ehm-meh]
the ATM

l'ufficio cambi
[loof-fee-choh cahm-bee]
the foreign exchange office

Vorrei...
[vohr-reh-ee]
I'd like to …

organizzare un trasferimento
[ohr-gah-nee-dzah-reh oon trahs-feh-ree-mehn-toh]
arrange a transfer

incassare un assegno
[een-cahs-sah-reh oon ahs-seh-nyoh]
cash a cheque

cambiare del denaro
[cahm-bee-ah-reh dehl deh-nah-roh]
change money

avere un anticipo in contanti
[ah-veh-reh oon ahn-tee-chee-poh een cohn-tahn-tee]
get a cash advance

prelevare del denaro
[preh-leh-vah-reh dehl deh-nah-roh]
withdraw money

Qual è...?
[qwah-leh]
What's …?

la tariffa per quello
[lah tah-reef-fah pehr qwehl-loh]
the charge for that

il tasso di cambio
[eel tahs-soh dee cahm-byoh]
the exchange rate

sono ... euro
[soh-noh... eh-oo-roh]
it's ... euros

è gratuito
[eh grah-too-ee-toh]
it's free

è già arrivato il mio denaro?
[eh djah ahr-ree-vah-toh eel mee-oh deh-nah-roh]
Has my money arrived yet?

Chapter 53: Paying / I pagamenti

il conto
[eel cohn-toh]
the bill (restaurant)

la ricevuta
[lah ree-cheh-voo-tah]
the bill (hotel)

la fattura
[lah faht-tooh-rah]
the invoice

la cassa
[lah cahs-sah]
the desk

Quanto costa?
[qwahn-toh coh-stah]
How much is it?

Quanto costerà?
[qwahn-toh coh-steh-rah]
How much will it be?

Posso pagare...?
[pohs-soh pah-gah-reh]
Can I pay...?

con carta di credito
[cohn cahr-tah dee creh-dee-toh]
by credit card

con assegno
[cohn ahs-seh-nyoh]
by cheque

lo metta sul mio conto
[loh meht-tah sool mee-oh cohn-toh]
Put it on my bill (hotel)

Dove pago?
[doh-veh pah-goh]
Where do I pay?

Accettate carte di credito?
[ah-tchet-tah-teh cahr-teh dee creh-dee-toh]
Do you take credit cards?

Il servizio è incluso?
[eel sehr-vee-tsyoh eh een-cloo-soh]
Is service included?

Può darmi lo scontrino, per favore?
[pwoh dahr-mee loh scohn-tree-noh, pehr fah-voh-reh]
Could you give me a receipt, please?

Pago in anticipo?
[pah-goh een ahn-tee-chee-poh]
Do I pay in advance?

Mi dispiace
[mee dee-spyah-cheh]
I'm sorry

non ho soldi spiccioli
[nohn hoh sohl-dee spee-tcho-lee]
I've nothing smaller (no change)

Chapter 54: Luggage / I bagagli

ritiro bagagli
[ree-tee-roh bah-gah-lee]
baggage reclaim

deposito bagagli
[deh-poh-see-toh bah-gah-lee]
left luggage

trolley
[troll-leh-ee]
luggage trolley

Il mio bagaglio non è ancora arrivato
[eel mee-oh bah-gah-lee-oh nohn eh ahn-coh-rah ahr-ree-vah-toh]
My luggage hasn't arrived yet

la mia valigia è stata danneggiata in volo
[lah mee-ah vah-lee-djah eh stah-tah dahn-neh-djah-tah een voh-loh]
My suitcase has been damaged on the flight

Chapter 55: Repairs / Riparazioni

Calzolaio
[cahl-tsoh-lah-yoh]
shoe repairer

è rotto
[eh roht-toh]
This is broken

Dove posso farlo riparare?
[doh-veh pohs-soh fahr-loh ree-pah-rah-reh]
Where can I get this repaired?

Può aggiustare...?
[pwoh ah-djoo-stah-reh]
Can you repair...?

queste scarpe
[qweh-steh scahr-peh]
these shoes

il mio orologio
[eel mee-oh oh-roh-loh-djoh]
my watch

i miei occhiali
[ee mee-eh-ee oh-kee-ah-lee]
my glasses

quanto tempo occorre?
[qwan-toh tehm-poh oh-cohr-reh]
How long will it take?

potrebbe riparare il mio ...?
[poh-trehb-beh ree-pah-rah-reh eel mee-oh]
Can I have my ... repaired?

è difettoso
[eh dee-feht-toh-soh]
It's faulty

Chapter 56: Laundry / Lavanderia

Tintoria
[teen-toh-ree-ah]
dry-cleaner's

lavanderia/ lavanderia a gettoni
[lah-vahn-deh-ree-ah/ lah-vahn-deh-ree-ah ah djet-toh-nee]
Launderette/ laundromat

detersivo in polvere
[deh-tehr-see-voh een pohl-veh-reh]
washing powder

stirare
[stee-rah-reh]
ironing

Chapter 57: Shopping / acquisti

Voglio fare shopping
[voh-lyoh fah-reh shopping]
I want to go shopping

mi piace quello
[mee pyah-tcheh qwehl-loh]
I like that

Quanto costa?
[qwahn-toh coh-stah]
How much is it?

è molto costoso
[eh mohl-toh coh-stoh-soh]
It is very expensive

preferisco qualcosa di migliore (più economico)
[preh-feh-rees-coh qwal-coh-sah dee mee-lyoh-reh (pyoo eh-coh-noh-mee-coh)]
I prefer something better (cheaper)

ne avete altri?
[neh ah-veh-teh ahl-tree]
Do you have any others?

può mostrarmene altri?
[pwoh moh-strahr-meh-neh ahl-tree]
Show me some others

posso provarlo?
[pohs-soh proh-vahr-loh]
May I try this on?

posso ordinarne uno?
[pohs-soh ohr-dee-nahr-neh oo-noh]
Can I order one?

per favore prenda le mie misure
[pehr fah-voh reh prehn-dah leh mee-eh mee-soo-reh]
Please take my measurements

Può spedirlo a New York?
[pwoh speh-deer-loh ah New York]
Can you ship it to New York City?

Può spedirlo all'estero?
[pwoh speh-deer-loh ahl-leh-steh-roh]
Can I have it sent overseas?

A chi pago?
[ah kee pah-goh]
Whom do I pay?

mi invii il conto
[mee een-vee eel cohn-toh]
Please bill me

voglio comprare una cuffia da bagno
[voh-lee-oh cohm-prah-reh oo-nah coof-fyah dah bah-nyoh]
I want to buy a bathing cap

un costume da bagno
[oon coh-stoo-meh dah bah-nyoh]
A bathing suit

un reggiseno
[oon reh-djee-seh-noh]
A brassiere

un abito
[oon ah-bee-toh]
A dress

un abito
[oon ah-bee-toh]
A suit

una camicetta
[oo-nah cah-mee-chet-tah]
A blouse

un cappotto
[oon cah-pot-toh]
A coat

un paio di guanti
[oon pah-yoh dee gwahn-tee]
A pair of gloves

una borsa
[oo-nah bohr-sah]
A handbag

dei fazzoletti
[deh-ee fah-tsoh-leht-tee]
some handkerchiefs

un cappello
[oon cahp-pehl-loh]
a hat

una giacca
[oo-nah djak-cah]
a jacket

della biancheria intima
[dehl-lah bee-ahn-keh-ree-ah een-tee-mah]
some lingerie

della biancheria intima
[dehl-lah bee-ahn-keh-ree-ah een-tee-mah]
some underwear

una camicia da notte
[oo-nah cah-mee-tcha dah noht-teh]
a nightgown

un impermeabile
[oon eem-pehr-meh-ah-bee-leh]
a raincoat

un paio di scarpe
[oon pah-yoh dee scahr-peh]
a pair of shoes

dei lacci
[deh-ee lah-tchee]
some shoelaces

un paio di pantofole
[oon pah-yoh dee pahn-toh-foh-leh]
a pair of slippers

un paio di calze
[oon pah-yoh dee cahl-tseh]
a pair of socks

un paio di collant
[oon pah-yoh dee cohl-lahnt]
a pair nylon

un maglione
[oon mah-lyoh-neh]
a sweater

delle cravatte
[dehl-leh crah-vaht-teh]
some ties

pantaloni
[pahn-tah-loh-nee]
trousers

Avete dei posacenere?
[ah-veh-teh deh-ee poh-sah-cheh-neh-reh]
Do you have some ashtrays?

una scatola di dolci
[oo-nah scah-toh-lah dee dohl-chee]
A box of candy

della porcellana
[dehl-lah pohr-tchel-lah-nah]
some porcelain

delle bambole
[dehl-leh bahm-boh-leh]
some dolls

degli orecchini
[deh-lee oh-reh-kee-nee]
some earings

del profumo
[dehl proh-foo-moh]
some perfume

dei quadri
[deh-ee qwah-dree]
some pictures

dei dischi
[deh-ee dees-kee]
some records

dell'argenteria
[dehl-lahr-djen-teh-ree-ah]
some silverware

dei giocattoli
[deh-ee djoh-caht-toh-lee]
some toys

un ombrello
[oon ohm-brehl-loh]
an umbrella

un orologio
[oon oh-roh-loh-djoh]
a watch

una cinta
[oo-nah cheen-tah]
a belt

dov'è...?
[doh-veh]
Where's ...?

la libreria
[lah lee-breh-ree-ah]
the bookshop

il grande magazzino
[eel grahn-deh mah-gah-dzee-noh]
the department store

il supermercato
[eel soo-pehr-mehr-cah-toh]
the grocery store

il supermercato
[eel soo-pehr-mehr-cah-toh]
the supermarket

l'edicola
[leh-dee-coh-lah]
the newsagency

dove posso comprare (un lucchetto)?
[doh-veh pohs-soh cohm-prah-reh (oon look-keh-toh)]
where can I buy (a padlock)?

sto cercando...
[stoh cher-cahn-doh]
I'm looking for ...

posso vederlo?
[pohs-soh veh-dehr-loh]
Can I look at it?

ha la garanzia?
[ah lah gah-rahn-tsee-ah]
Does it have a guarantee?

per favore, vorrei...
[pehr fah-voh-reh, voh-reh-ee]
I'd like ..., please.

una busta
[oo-nah boo-stah]
a bag

un rimborso
[oon reem-bohr-soh]
a refund

restituire questo
[reh-stee-too-ee-reh qweh-stoh]
to return this

Potrebbe scrivere il prezzo?
[poh-treh-beh scree-veh-reh eel preh-tsoh]
Can you write down the price?

Può ridurre il prezzo?
[pwoh ree-doo-reh eel preh-tsoh]
Can you lower the price?

Le darò (cinque) euro
[leh dah-roh (cheen-qweh) eh-oo-roh]
I'll give you (five) euros

C'è un errore nel conto
[cheh oon eh-roh-reh nehl cohn-toh]
There's a mistake in the bill

Chapter 58: To Complain / Lamentarsi

non funziona
[nohn foon-tsee-oh-nah]
This doesn't work

è sporco
[eh spohr-coh]
It's dirty

la luce
[lah loo-cheh]
light

la serratura
[lah sehr-rah-too-rah]
lock

il riscaldamento
[eel rees-cahl-dah-mehn-toh]
heating

l'aria condizionata
[lah-ree-ah con-dee-tsyoh-nah-tah]
air conditioning

è rotto
[eh rott-toh]
It's broken

voglio un rimborso
[voh-lee-oh oon reem-bohr-soh]
I want a refund

Chapter 59: Problems / Problemi

Può aiutarmi?
[pwoh ah-yoo-tahr-mee]
Can you help me?

Parlo poco italiano
[pahr-loh poh-coh ee-tah-lyah-noh]
I speak very little Italian

Qualcuno qui parla inglese?
[qwahl-coo-noh qwee pahr-lah een-gleh-seh]
Does anyone here speak English?

Vorrei parlare con il responsabile
[voh-reh-ee pahr-lah-reh cohn eel reh-spohn-sah-bee-leh]
I would like to speak to whoever is in charge

Mi sono perso
[mee soh-noh pehr-soh]
I'm lost

Come arrivo a...?
[coh-meh ah-ree-voh ah]
How do I get to…?

ho perso...
[oh pehr-soh]
I missed…

il mio treno
[eel myoh treh-noh]
my train

il mio volo
[eel myoh voh-loh]
my plane

la mia coincidenza
[lah mee-ah coh-een-chee-dehn-tsah]
my connection

Ho perso il mio volo perché c'era uno sciopero
[oh pehr-soh eel myoh voh-loh pehr-keh che-rah oo-noh shoh-peh-roh]
I've missed my flight because there was a strike

Può mostrarmi come funziona?
[pwoh moss-trahr-mee coh-meh foon-tsyoh-nah]
Can you show me how this works?

Ho perso il mio portafoglio
[hoh pehr-soh eel myoh pohr-tah-foh-lyoh]
I have lost my purse

ho bisogno di andare a ...
[hoh bee-soh-nyoh dee ahn-dah-reh ah]
I need to get to…

lasciatemi solo!
[lah-shah-teh-mee soh-loh]
leave me alone!

Andate via!
[ahn-dah-teh vee-ah]
Go away!

Chapter 60: Emergencies / Emergenze

La prego, chiami
[lah preh-goh, kyah-mee]
Please call

la polizia
[lah poh-lee-tsee-ah]
the police

un'ambulanza
[oon ahm-boo-lahn-tsah]
an ambulance

i vigili del fuoco
[ee vee-djee-lee dehl fwoh-coh]
fire brigade

la stazione di polizia
[lah stah-tsee-oh neh dee poh-lee-tsee-ah]
police station

Dov'è la stazione di polizia?
[doh-veh lah stah-tsee-oh neh dee poh-lee-tsee-ah]
Where is the police station?

pronto soccorso
[prohn-toh soh-cohr-soh]
accident and emergency department

Aiuto!
[ah-yoo-toh]
Help!

Al fuoco!
[ahl fwoh-coh]
Fire!

può aiutarmi?
[pwoh ah-yoo-tahr-mee]
Can you help me?

C'è stato un incidente
[cheh stah-toh oon een-chee-dehn-teh]
There has been an accident

qualcuno è stato ferito
[qwal-coo-noh eh stah-toh feh-ree-toh]
Someone has been injured

Vorrei denunciare un furto
[voh-reh-ee deh-noon-chah-reh oon foor-toh]
I want to report a theft

sono stato derubato/attaccato
[soh-noh stah-toh deh-roo-bah-toh/ah-tah-kah-toh]
I've been robbed/ attacked

sono stata stuprata
[soh-noh stah-tah stoo-prah-tah]
I've been raped

voglio parlare con un'agente di polizia donna
[voh-lyoh pahr-lah-reh cohn uhn ah-djehn-teh dee poh-lee-tsee-ah dohn-nah]
I want to speak to a policewoman

hanno rubato...
[hah-noh roo-bah-toh]
Someone has stolen…

la mia borsa
[lah mee-ah bohr-sah]
my handbag

i miei soldi
[ee mee-eh-ee sohl-dee]
my money

Chapter 60: Emergencies / Emergenze

la mia auto è stata aperta
[lah mee-ah ah-oo-toh eh stah-tah ah-pehr-tah]
My car has been broken into

la mia auto è stata rubata
[lah mee-ah ah-oo-toh eh stah-tah roo-bah-tah]
My car has been stolen

ho bisogno di fare una telefonata
[hoh bee-soh-nyoh dee fah-reh oo-nah teh-leh-foh-nah-tah]
I need to make a telephone call

mi serve un verbale per la mia assicurazione
[mee sehr-veh oon vehr-bah-leh pehr la mee-ah ah-see-coo-rah-tsyoh-neh]
need a report for my insurance

non conoscevo il limite di velocità
[non coh-noh-sheh-voh eel lee-mee-teh dee veh-loh-chee-tah]
I didn't know the speed limit

quant'è la multa?
[qwahn-teh lah mool-tah]
How much is the fine?

dove posso pagarla?
[doh-veh poh-soh pah-gahr-lah]
Where do I pay it?

devo pagarla subito?
[deh-voh pah-gahr-lah soo-bee-toh]
Do I have to pay it straight away?

mi dispiace agente
[mee dees-pyah-cheh, ah-jen-teh]
I'm very sorry, officer

lei è passato con il rosso
[leh-ee eh pahs-sah-toh cohn eel rohs-soh]
You went through a red light

lei non ha dato la precedenza
[leh-ee non hah dah-toh lah preh-tcheh-dehn-tsah]
You didn't give way

Part 8 : Health – La salute

If you are traveling to an Italian-speaking country, you will need to know some health-related vocabulary. Whether you require pain-killers from the pharmacy or have an emergency doctor's visit while abroad, you will likely encounter health-related situations and it is an invaluable skill to be able to speak the necessary Italian to navigate such issues.

Chapter 61: Pharmacy / La farmacia

la farmacia
[la fahr-mah-chee-ah]
pharmacy

la farmacia di turno
[la fahr-mah-chee-ah dee toor-noh]
duty chemist's

Può darmi qualcosa per...?
[pwoh dahr-mee qwahl-coh-sah pehr]
Can you give me something for…?

il mal di testa
[eel mahl dee teh-stah]
a headache

il mal d'auto
[eel mahl dah-oo-toh]
car sickness

l'influenza
[leen-floo-ehn-tsah]
flu

la diarrea
[lah dee-ah-reh-ah]
diarrhea

le scottature
[leh scott-tah-too-reh]
sunburn

è adatto per bambini?
[eh ah-dah-toh pehr ee bahm-bee-nee]
Is it safe for children?

Quanto devo dargliene?
[qwahn-toh deh-voh dahr-lee-eh-neh]
How much should I give him/her?

Chapter 62: Dealing with Medical Issues / Problemi di salute

un dentista
[oon dehn-tees-tah]
a dentist

un dottore
[oon doc-toh-reh]
a doctor

un ospedale
[oon oh-speh-dah-leh]
a hospital

una farmacia (notturna)
[oo-nah fahr-mah-chee-ah (noh-toor-nah)]
a (night) pharmacist

Ho bisogno di un medico (che parli inglese)
[hoh bee-soh-nyoh dee oon doc-toh-reh (keh pahr-lee een-gleh-seh)]
I need a doctor (who speaks English).

potrei vedere una dottoressa?
[poh-treh-ee veh-deh-reh oo-nah doc-toh-reh-tsah]
Could I see a female doctor?

ho finito le mie medicine
[hoh fee-nee-toh leh mee-eh meh-dee-chee-neh]
I've run out of my medication

sono malato
[soh-noh mah-lah-toh]
I'm sick.

mi fa male qui
[mee fah mah-leh qwee]
It hurts here.

Io ho...
[ee-oh hoh]
I have (a) ...

l'asma
[lahs-mah]
asthma

la bronchite
[lah brohn-kee-teh]
bronchitis

la stipsi
[lah steep-seeh]
constipation

la tosse
[lah tohs-seh]
cough

la diarrea
[lah dee-ah-reh-ah]
diarrhea

la febbre
[lah feh-breh]
fever

il mal di testa
[eel mahl dee teh-stah]
headache

problemi di cuore
[proh-bleh-mee dee qwoh-reh]
heart condition

la nausea
[lah nah-oo-seh-ah]
nausea

dolore
[doh-loh-reh]
pain

la gola infiammata
[lah goh-lah een-fee-ah-mah-tah]
sore throat

mal di denti
[mahl dee dehn-tee]
toothache

sono allergico...
[soh-noh ahl-lehr-djee-coh]
I'm allergic to...

agli antibiotici
[ahl-lee ahn-tee-byoh-tee-chee]
antibiotics

agli antinfiammatori
[ah-lee ahn-tee-een-fee-ahm-mah-toh-ree]
anti-inflammatories

agli antidolorifici
[ah-lee ahn-tee-doh-loh-ree-fee-chee]
painkillers

all'aspirina
[ah-lah-spee-ree-nah]
aspirin

alle api
[ah-leh ah-pee]
bees

alla codeina
[ahl-lah co-deh-ee-nah]
codeine

alla penicellina
[ahl-lah peh-nee-chell-lee-nah]
penicillin

all'antisettico
[ahl-lahn-tee-sett-tee-coh]
antiseptic

bende
[behn-deh]
bandage

preservativi
[preh-sehr-vah-tee-vee]
condoms

contraccettivi
[cohn-trah-tchet-tee-vee]
contraceptives

repellente per insetti
[reh-pehl-lehn-teh pehr een-seht-teeh]
insect repellent

lassativi
[lah-tsah-tee-vee]
laxatives

sali di reidratazione
[sah-lee dee reh-eee-drah-tah-tsyoh-neh]
rehydration salts

sonniferi
[sohn-nee-feh-ree]
sleeping tablets

vorrei vedere un dottore americano
[vohr-reh-ee veh-deh-reh oon doc-toh-reh ah-meh-ree-cah-noh]
I wish to see an American doctor

non dormo bene
[nohn dohr-moh beh-neh]
I do not sleep well

mi fa male la testa
[mee fah mah-leh lah teh-stah]
My head aches

devo restare a letto?
[deh-voh reh-stah-reh ah leht-toh]
Must I stay In bed?

posso alzarmi?
[pohs-soh ahl-zahr-mee]
May I get up?

mi sento meglio
[mee sehn-toh meh-lee-oh]
I feel better

Chapter 63: Doctor / Il dottore

ospedale
[oh-speh-dah-leh]
hospital

pronto soccorso
[prohn-toh soh-cohr-soh]
accident and emergency department

consultazioni
[cohn-sool-tah-tsyoh-nee]
consultations

mi sento male
[mee sehn-toh mah-leh]
I feel ill

Ha la febbre?
[hah lah feh-breh]
Do you have a temperature?

No, mi fa male qui
[noh, mee fah mah-leh qwee]
No, I have a pain here

mi serve un medico
[mee sehr-veh oon meh-dee-coh]
I need a doctor

mio figlio/mia figlia è malato/a
[mee-oh fee-lyoh/mee-ah fee-lyah eh mah-lah-toh/mah-lah-tah]
My son/My daughter is ill

sono diabetico
[soh-noh dee-ah-beh-tee-coh]
I'm diabetic

sono incinta
[soh-noh een-cheen-tah]
I'm pregnant

prendo la pillola
[prehn-doh lah peel-loh-lah]
I'm on the pill

mi serve la ricevuta per l'assicurazione
[mee sehr-veh lah ree-cheh-voo-tah pehr lah-see-coo-rah-tsyoh-neh]
I need a receipt for the insurance

Chapter 64: Dentist / Il dentista

Ho bisogno di un dentista
[hoh bee-soh-nyoh dee oon dehn-tee-stah]
I need to see a dentist

Ha mal di denti
[hah mahl dee dehn-tee]
He/She has toothache

Può fare un'otturazione temporanea?
[pwoh fah-reh oon ott-too-rah-tsyoh-neh tehm-poh-rah-neh-ah]
Can you do a temporary filling?

Può darmi qualcosa per il dolore?
[pwoh dahr-mee qwahl-coh-sah pehr eel doh-loh-reh]
Can you give me something for the pain?

Fa male
[fah mah-leh]
It hurts

Può riparare la mia dentiera?
[pwoh ree-pah-rah-reh lah mee-ah dehn-tee-eh-rah]
Can you repair my dentures?

Devo pagare?
[deh-voh pah-gah-reh]
Do I have to pay?

Quanto costerà?
[qwahn-toh coh-steh-rah]
How much will it be?

mi serve la ricevuta per l'assicurazione
[mee sehr-veh lah ree-cheh-voo-tah pehr lah-see-coo-rah-tsyoh-neh]
I need a receipt for the insurance

Part 9: Miscellaneous / Varie

If you want more additional phrases ☺

Chapter 65: Liquid / I liquidi

mezzo litro di
[med-zoh lee-troh dee...]
1/2 litre of

un litro di
[oon lee-troh dee...]
a litre of

mezza bottiglia di
[med-zah boh-tee-lyah dee]
1/2 bottle of

una bottiglia di
[oo-nah boh-tee-lyah dee]
a bottle of

un bicchiere di
[oon bee-kee-eh-reh dee]
a glass of

Chapter 66: Quantity / Quantità

100 grammi di
[chen-toh grahm-mee dee]
100 grams of

un etto di
[oon eht-toh dee]
100 grams of

mezzo chilo di
[med-zoh kee-loh dee]
a half kilo of…

un kilo di
[oon kee-loh dee]
a kilo of

una fetta di
[oo-nah feht-tah dee]
a slice of

una porzione di
[oo-nah pohr-tsyoh-neh dee]
a portion of

una dozzina
[oo-nah doh-zee-nah]
a dozen

una scatola di
[oo-nah scah-toh-lah dee]
a box of

un pacchetto di
[oon pah-ket-toh dee]
a packet of

un cartone di
[oon cahr-toh-neh dee]
a carton of

un barattolo di
[oon bah-raht-toh-loh dee]
a jar of

500 euro di
[cheen-qweh-chen-toh e-oo-roh dee]
500 euros of

un quarto
[oon qwahr-toh]
a quarter

dieci per cento
[dee-eh-chee pehr chen-toh]
ten per cent

più...
[pyoo]
more...

meno...
[meh-noh]
less...

abbastanza di...
[ah-bah-stahn-tsah dee]
enough of...

il doppio
[eel dohp-pyoh]
double

due volte
[doo-eh vohl-teh]
twice

una volta
[oo-nah vohl-tah]
once

Chapter 67: Cardinal numbers / I numeri cardinali

zero
[zeh-roh]
0

Uno
[oo-noh]
1

due
[doo-eh]
2

tre
[treh]
3

Quattro
[qwah-troh]
4

Cinque
[cheen-qweh]
5

sei
[seh-ee]
6

sette
[seht-teh]
7

otto
[oht-toh]
8

nove
[noh-veh]
9

dieci
[dee-eh-chee]
10

Undici
[oon-dee-chee]
11

Dodici
[doh-dee-chee]
12

Tredici
[treh-dee-chee]
13

quattordici
[qwah-tohr-dee-chee]
14

quindici
[qween-dee-chee]
15

Sedici
[seh-dee-chee]
16

diciassette
[dee-chah-seht-teh]
17

Diciotto
[dee-chot-toh]
18

diciannove
[dee-chan-noh-veh]
19

venti
[vehn-tee]
20

ventuno
[vehn-too-noh]
21

ventidue
[vehn-tee-doo-eh]
22

Ventitré
[vehn-tee-treh]
23

Trenta
[trehn-tah]
30

trentuno
[trehn-too-noh]
31

trentadue
[trehn-tah-doo-eh]
32

quaranta
[qwah-rahn-tah]
40

Quarantuno
[qwah-rahn-too-noh]
41

Quarantadue
[qwah-rahn-tah-doo-eh]
42

cinquanta
[cheen-qwahn-tah]
50

Sessanta
[seh-sahn-tah]
60

Settanta
[seht-tahn-tah]
70

Ottanta
[ott-tahn-tah]
80

Novanta
[noh-vahn-tah]
90

Cento
[chen-toh]
100

centodieci
[chen-toh-dee-eh-chee]
110

Duecento
[doo-eh-chen-toh]
200

Duecentocinquanta
[doo-eh-chen-toh-cheen-qwahn-tah]
250

Mille
[meel-leh]
1000

un milione
[oon mee-lyoh-neh]
1 million

Chapter 68: Time / L'ora

Che ora è?
[keh oh-rah eh]
What time is it?

sono...
[soh-noh...]
It's...

le due
[leh doo-eh]
two o'clock

le tre
[leh treh]
three o'clock

è l'una
[eh loo-nah]
It's one o'clock

è mezzanotte
[eh meh-dzah-not-teh]
It's midnight

le nove e dieci
[leh noh-veh eh dee-eh-chee]
9,10

le nove e un quarto
[leh noh-veh eh oon qwahr-toh]
quarter past 9

le nove e mezza
[leh noh-veh eh meh-tsah]
9,30

le nove e trentacinque
[leh noh-veh eh trehn-tah-cheen-qweh]
9,35

le dieci meno un quarto
[leh dee-eh-chee meh-noh oon qwahr-toh]
quarter to 10

le dieci meno dieci
[leh dee-eh-chee meh-noh dee-eh-chee]
10 to 10

A che ora...?
[ah keh oh-rah...]
When does it...?

apre/chiude/inizia/finisce
[ah-preh/kyoo-deh/ee-nee-tsyah/fee-nee-sheh]
open/close/begin/finish

alle tre
[ahl-leh treh]
at three o'clock

prima delle tre
[pree-mah dehl-leh treh]
before three o'clock

dopo le tre
[doh-poh leh treh]
after three o'clock

oggi
[oh-djee]
today

stasera
[stah-seh-rah]
tonight

domani
[doh-mah-nee]
tomorrow

ieri
[yeh-ree]
yesterday

avant'ieri
[ah-vahn-tee-yeh-ree]
the day before yesterday

la scorsa notte
[lah scohr-sah nott-teh]
last night

dopodomani
[doh-poh-doh-mah-nee]
the day after tomorrow

la mattina/il mattino
[lah mah-tee-nah/eel mah-tee-noh]
the morning

il pomeriggio
[eel poh-meh-ree-djoh]
the afternoon

la sera
[lah seh-rah]
the evening

la notte
[lah nott-teh]
the night

la prossima settimana
[lah pross-see-mah seht-tee-mah-nah]
next week

la scorsa settimana
[lah scohr-sah seht-tee-mah-nah]
last week

questo mese
[qweh-stoh meh-seh]
this month

Chapter 69: Days of the week / I giorni della settimana

Lunedì
[loo-neh-dee]
Monday

Martedì
[mar-teh-dee]
Tuesday

Mercoledì
[mehr-coh-leh-dee]
Wednesday

Giovedì
[djoh-veh-dee]
Thursday

Venerdì
[veh-nehr-dee]
Friday

Sabato
[sah-bah-toh]
Saturday

Domenica
[doh-meh-nee-cah]
Sunday

Chapter 70: Months of the year / I mesi dell'anno

Gennaio
[jen-nah-yoh]
January

Febbraio
[feb-brah-yoh]
February

Marzo
[mar-tsoh]
March

Aprile
[ah-pree-leh]
April

Maggio
[mah-djoh]
May

Giugno
[joo-nyoh]
June

Luglio
[loo-lyoh]
July

Agosto
[ah-goh-stoh]
August

Settembre
[set-tehm-breh]
September

Ottobre
[ott-toh-breh]
October

Novembre
[noh-vehm-breh]
November

Dicembre
[dee-chem-breh]
December

Chapter 71: Seasons / Le stagioni

Primavera
[pree-mah-veh-rah]
spring

estate
[eh-stah-teh]
summer

autunno
[ah-oo-toon-noh]
autumn

inverno
[een-vehr-noh]
winter

Chapter 72: Colors & Shapes / Colori e Forme

verde
[vehr-deh]
green

blu
[bloo]
blue

celeste
[cheh-leh-steh]

light blue

rosso
[rohs-soh]
red

nero
[neh-roh]
black

rosa
[roh-sah]
pink

bianco
[byahn-coh]
white

arancione
[ah-rahn-choh-neh]
orange

giallo
[djah-loh]
yellow

grigio
[gree-djoh]
grey

viola
[vyoh-lah]
purple

marrone
[mah-roh-neh]
brown

cerchio
[cher-kyoh]
circle

quadrato
[qwah-drah-toh]
square

rettangolo
[rett-tahn-goh-loh]
rectangle

rombo
[rom-boh]
rhombus

triangolo
[tree-ahn-goh-loh]
triangle

cubo
[coo-boh]
cube

Chapter 73: Measurements / Misure

Qual è la lunghezza?
[qwah-leh lah loon-gweh-tsah]
What Is the length?

La larghezza
[lah lahr-gweh-tsah]
The width

La taglia
[lah tah-lyah]
The size

Altezza
[ahl-teh-tsah]
Height

Quant'è al metro?
[qwahn-teh ahl meh-troh]
How much is it per meter?

è 10 metri di lunghezza per 4 di larghezza
[eh dee-eh-chee meh-tree dee loon-gweh-tsah pehr qwah-troh dee lahr-gweh-tsah]
It is ten meters long by four meters wide

Alto
[ahl-toh]
High

Basso
[bahs-soh]
Low

Largo
[lahr-goh]
Large

Piccolo
[peek-koh-loh]
Small

Medio
[meh-dyoh]
Medium

Simile
[see-mee-leh]
Alike

Diverso
[dee-vehr-soh]
Different

Un paio
[oon pah-yoh]
A pair

Una dozzina
[oo-nah doh-tsee-nah]
A dozen

Una mezza dozzina
[oo-nah meh-dzah doh-tsee-nah]
A half dozen

Conclusion

Italian is an incredibly beautiful language to learn. Whether you're learning these phrases as a way to boost your Italian language studies or to help you enjoy your Italian holiday, we hope this book was able to help you achieve your goals.

If you have a few minutes to spare, please let us know your thoughts about this book by sending an email to contact@talkinitalian.com. We'd be delighted to receive any feedback from you. Any suggestions on how we could further improve this book will be very much welcome. My team and I are always looking for ways to improve our products so that they can be of greater help to language learners like you.

For more insights about the Italian language and culture, do visit our website at Talkinitalian.com. We are always working towards providing useful content for you.

And so with that, we say our goodbyes.

Grazie.

The Talk in Italian Team

Audio Download Instructions

- Copy and paste this link into your browser:

    https://talkinitalian.com/download-italian-phrasebook/

- Click on the book cover. It will take you to a Dropbox folder containing each individual file. (If you're not familiar with what Dropbox is or how it works, don't panic, it just a storage facility.)
- Click the download button in the Dropbox folder located in the upper right portion of your screen. A box may pop up asking you to sign in to Dropbox. Simply click, "No thanks, continue to download" under the sign in boxes. (If you have a Dropbox account, you can choose to save it to your own Dropbox so you have access anywhere via the internet.)
- The files you have downloaded will be saved in a .zip file. Note: This is large file. Don't try opening it until your browser tells you that it has completed the download successfully (usually a few minutes on a broadband connection but if your connection is unreliable, it could take 10 to 20 minutes).
- The files will be in your "downloads" folder unless you have changed your settings. Extract them from the folder and save them to your computer or copy to your preferred devices, et voilà ! You can now listen to the audio anytime, anywhere.

I am Here to Help

J'adore my language and culture and would love to share it with you.

Should you have any questions regarding my book, the French language and culture, or technical issues, I am happy to answer them. You can contact me via email or through the Talk in French Facebook page.

Email: contact@talkinitalian.com
Facebook: facebook.com/talkininitalian